FND

ACPL ITEM
DISCARDED

NONPROFIT
RESOURCE CENTER

D1457854

How to Calculate
the Public Support Test

THIRD EDITION

Kelly Shipp Simone

COUNCIL *on* FOUNDATIONS

APR 5 2007

Vision

The Council's vision for the field is of

A vibrant, growing and responsible philanthropic sector that advances the common good.

We see ourselves as part of a broad philanthropic community that will contribute to this vision. We aim to be an important leader in reaching the vision.

Mission

The Council on Foundations provides the opportunity, leadership and tools needed by philanthropic organizations to expand, enhance and sustain their ability to advance the common good.

To carry out this mission, we will be a membership organization with effective and diverse leadership that helps the field be larger, more effective, more responsible and more cooperative.

By "*common good,*" we mean the sum total of conditions that enable community members to thrive. These achievements have a shared nature that goes beyond individual benefits.

By "*philanthropic organizations,*" we mean any vehicle that brings people together to enhance the effectiveness, impact and leverage of their philanthropy. This includes private and community foundations, corporate foundations and giving programs, operating foundations and public foundations, as well as emerging giving and grantmaking mechanisms involving collective participation.

Statement of Inclusiveness

The Council on Foundations was formed to promote responsible and effective philanthropy. The mission requires a commitment to inclusiveness as a fundamental operating principle and calls for an active and ongoing process that affirms human diversity in its many forms, encompassing but not limited to ethnicity, race, gender, sexual orientation, economic circumstance, disability and philosophy. We seek diversity in order to ensure that a range of perspectives, opinions and experiences are recognized and acted upon in achieving the Council's mission. The Council also asks members to make a similar commitment to inclusiveness in order to better enhance their abilities to contribute to the common good of our changing society.

© 2006 Council on Foundations, Inc. All rights reserved.

This publication may not be reproduced without attribution to *How to Calculate the Public Support Test* and the Council on Foundations. Revenue from publications sales supports the Council on Foundations and ensures its capacity to produce resources and provide services to promote responsible and effective philanthropy. Members of the Council on Foundations may obtain copies of this book and other Council publications at member rates by calling 888/239-5221.

Library of Congress Cataloging-in-Publication Data
Shipp Simone, Kelly.
 How to calculate the public support test / by Kelly Shipp Simone.—
Third ed.
  p. cm.
 Rev. ed. of.: How to calculate the public support test / by John A. Edie.
 ISBN 1-932677-28-3
 1. Charities—United States—Handbooks, manuals, etc. 2. Endowments—United States—Handbooks, manuals, etc.
3. Charitable uses, trusts, and foundations—United States—Handbooks, manuals, etc.
I. Edie, John A. How to calculate the public support test. II. Council on Foundations. III. Title.
 HV41.S47 2006
 658.15'224—dc22
      2006024142

COUNCIL *on* **FOUNDATIONS**
1828 L Street, NW, Suite 300
Washington, DC 20036-5168
202/466-6512 • Fax 202/785-3926
cof.org

TABLE OF CONTENTS

HOW TO CALCULATE THE PUBLIC SUPPORT TEST

FOREWORD

S ince the Tax Reform Act of 1969, the public support test has served as a crucial test for community foundations and other publicly supported charities to understand and apply as a means of maintaining good standing as a public charity. The Council has been assisting charities with understanding the test since the test's inception.

This revised edition of *How to Calculate the Public Support Test* reflects the increased sophistication in the activities of public charities in general and community foundations in particular. The revised edition builds upon the solid foundation established by the original 1998 version of this publication written by former Senior Vice President and General Counsel of the Council on Foundations John A. Edie.

In this publication, Kelly Shipp Simone, senior staff attorney, has taken a fresh look at the public support test and delved deeper into frequent issues for charities such as how to incorporate fundraising income into the test and how to account for contributions to and from donor-advised funds. You will also find more charts to help elucidate the concepts discussed in the text.

We thank the reviewers of this publication, Susan Nicholson of The Community Foundation of Louisville and Karen Hand of The Community Foundation Serving Richmond and Central Virginia, for their fresh take on the publication. We also thank the Legal Services and Standards department of the Council on Foundations, particularly Jane Nober, for reviewing and enhancing the publication throughout its production.

We hope this publication's user-friendly, step-by-step approach to the public support test will assist charity staff and managers and those professional lawyers and accountants who work with them.

Steve Gunderson

President and CEO
Council on Foundations

INTRODUCTION

Although individuals working with publicly supported charities typically recognize the importance of the public support test in maintaining public charity status, they often encounter questions as they try to apply the test to a charity's particular set of facts. This publication provides a convenient reference that explains the test and provides the tools to help calculate a charity's percentage of public support. Understanding the public support test takes time, yet it is not only possible but also important to do so.

Athough this publication provides a wealth of information about calculating the public support test, it is no substitute for advice from a lawyer or accountant familiar with the specific finances of a charity.

This book aims to provide even the most math phobic reader with the tools to understand the public support test. It opens with a brief historical background that helps to answer the questions: "Why does passing the public support test matter?" and "Why does the public support test exist?" A general introduction to the test (Chapter 1) is followed by a detailed breakdown of its parts (Chapters 2–6). Examples and charts throughout clarify the text. Chapter 7 covers the different ways that fundraising may affect an organization's public support calculation. Chapter 8 discusses the consequences of failing the test. The appendix includes Internal Revenue Service guidance materials and the Council on Foundations' explanations of them.

Importance of Passing the Public Support Test

In the United States, organizations that qualify to receive charitable tax-deductible contributions are described in Section 501(c)(3) of the Tax Code.[1] Section 501(c)(3) charitable organizations are divided into two main categories—public charities and private foundations. A charitable organization acquires two definite advantages if it can obtain a tax ruling from the Internal Revenue Service (IRS) classifying it as a public charity instead of a private foundation. First, gifts or contributions made by living donors to a public charity generally qualify for a higher federal charitable deduction than similar contributions to most private foundations. Second, public charities are not subject to the stricter regulations imposed on private foundations, including penalty taxes that can be applied to the foundation and to foundation managers.[2]

---

[1] All references to the Tax Code are to the Internal Revenue Code of 1986, as amended. All references to regulations are to the applicable Treasury Department regulations promulgated under the Internal Revenue Code.

[2] For a more detailed treatment of the distinctions between public and private foundations, see John A. Edie, *First Steps in Starting a Foundation*, 5th ed. (Washington, DC: Council on Foundations, 2002).

The IRS presumes that a charitable entity is a private foundation unless it can demonstrate that it should be classified as a public charity. Some organizations demonstrate that they are public charities by meeting a legal definition; churches, schools and medical institutions satisfy such definitions.[3] Other public charities acquire their public classification through their relationship with another publicly supported charity; these public charities are called supporting organizations.[4] But most public charities meet and maintain their public status by continually demonstrating that a certain minimum amount of their total support is "public support" and comes from a broad cross-section of the public, not from just one source (one person, one family, one foundation or one company). The law builds on the notion that if a charity depends on contributions or other support from the public, it will respond to that public and serve its charitable needs. If an organization does not qualify as a public charity based on meeting a definition, having a specified relationship with another publicly supported organization or passing a public support test, it will be deemed a private foundation.[5] (See Figure 1.) Although some organizations actively seek status as private foundations from inception, many more seek to demonstrate that they are public charities.

The Internal Revenue Code lists two different public support tests. Very generally, the first public support test relies on gifts and contributions, and the second test relies on gross receipts. This book will discuss *only the first of the two*—the test that relies primarily on gifts and contributions to meet the minimum percentage requirement and does *not* count gross receipts (admission fees, fees for services, etc.) as public support. In legal terms, the first type of publicly supported organization is defined under Sections 509(a)(1) and 170(b)(1)(A)(vi). Examples of organizations likely to qualify under this public support test include those with purposes to educate the public about issues such as education or the environment and direct service providers such as a domestic violence shelter or the American Red Cross. Almost without exception, community foundations maintain their public charity status under the first test.[6]

The second test, which *does* count gross receipts as public support, is generally more restrictive and is not included in this book. For example, under this second test, investment income cannot exceed one-third of total support, and all contributions from disqualified persons (such as members of the charity's board) do not count as public support. Organizations that rely on this public support test generally take in a sub-stantial proportion of their total support from admission fees. Examples of organizations likely to qualify under this public support test include symphonies, operas and theaters.[7]

New organizations in the process of obtaining recognition of tax-exempt status through the IRS will indicate to them whether the organization wishes to be a public charity or a private foundation when completing Form 1023, Application for Recognition of Exemption Under Section 501(c)(3) of the Internal

---

[3]   For example, a school (referred to as an educational organization) must demonstrate that it presents formal instruction as its primary func-tion as well as has a regularly scheduled curriculum, a faculty of qualified teachers, an enrolled student body and a place where educational activities are regularly carried on to qualify as a public charity under Treas. Reg. § 1.170A-9(b).

[4]   Because of the relationship between the supporting organization and another publicly supported charity, a supporting organization is not required to meet a public support test.

[5]   Organizations may also demonstrate that they qualify as a public charity by demonstrating that they are organized and operated for testing for public safety under § 509(a)(4). This method of achieving public charity status is infrequently used. See IRS Publication 557, *Tax-Exempt Status for Your Organization*.

[6]   In fact, the Council on Foundations and the National Standards for U.S. Community Foundations require that an organization be classified under § 509(a)(1) and § 170(b)(1)(A)(vi) to be considered a "community foundation."

[7]   In legal terms, this type of publicly supported organization is defined in § 509(a)(2). See *First Steps in Starting a Foundation*, pp. 11–12.

   © 2006, Council on Foundations, Inc.

Revenue Code. If public charity status is sought, the organization will also be required to indicate on Form 1023 how it qualifies as a public charity.[8]

To determine which test applies to an existing public charity, one should refer to the tax determination letter provided to the charity from the IRS. If this letter states that the charity is a Section 509(a)(1) organization and/or a Section 170(b)(1)(A)(vi) organization, the first test applies. If the letter states that the charity is a Section 509(a)(2) organization, the second test applies, and the discussion in this publication will not apply.[9]

To summarize: An organization may achieve public charity status by meeting a legal definition or a public support test or through some legally defined relationship with another publicly supported charity. An organization that does not meet any of these requirements may still be classified as a charitable organization but will be a private foundation.

---

[8] Churches, integrated auxiliaries of churches, and conventions and associations of churches are not required to apply to the IRS for recognition of their charity status. The term "churches" is used by the IRS generically to refer to similar religious institutions of other faiths such as synagogues and mosques. Similarly, organizations with gross receipts normally less than $5,000 in a tax year are not required to apply for recognition of exempt status.

[9] If the organization's determination letter does not include information indicating the organization's reason for public charity status or if the organization does not have its determination letter on file, the organization may request an updated letter that should provide this information. The IRS maintains a customer service number for questions about exempt organizations (877/829-5500). If the letter indicates that the organization is a § 509(a)(3) public charity, the organization is a "supporting organization." A designation of § 509(a)(4) indicates that the organization is a public charity because it is operated exclusively for testing for public safety.

FIGURE 1: SECTION 501(C)(3) ORGANIZATIONS

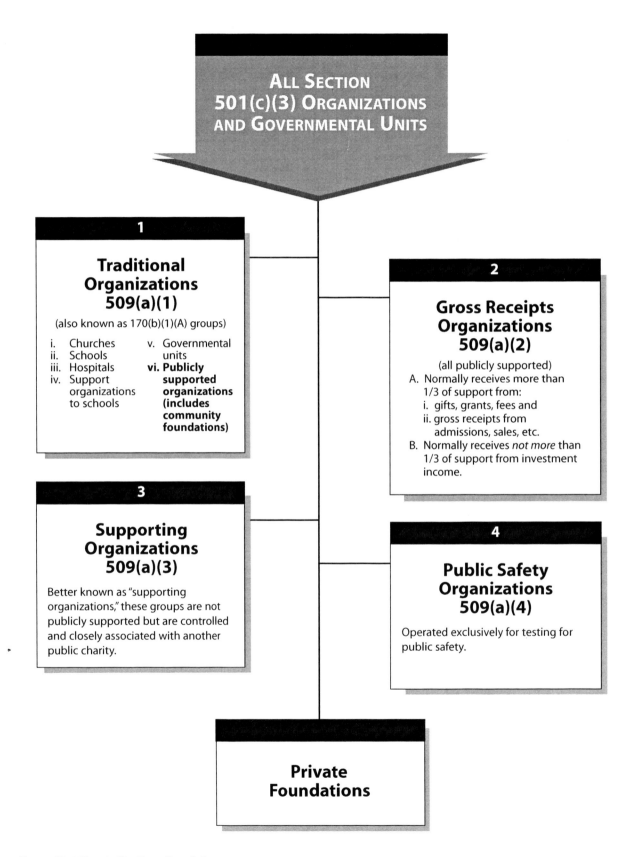

ALL SECTION 501(c)(3) ORGANIZATIONS AND GOVERNMENTAL UNITS

1
Traditional Organizations 509(a)(1)

(also known as 170(b)(1)(A) groups)

i. Churches
ii. Schools
iii. Hospitals
iv. Support organizations to schools
v. Governmental units
vi. **Publicly supported organizations (includes community foundations)**

2
Gross Receipts Organizations 509(a)(2)

(all publicly supported)
A. Normally receives more than 1/3 of support from:
  i. gifts, grants, fees and
  ii. gross receipts from admissions, sales, etc.
B. Normally receives *not more* than 1/3 of support from investment income.

3
Supporting Organizations 509(a)(3)

Better known as "supporting organizations," these groups are not publicly supported but are controlled and closely associated with another public charity.

4
Public Safety Organizations 509(a)(4)

Operated exclusively for testing for public safety.

Private Foundations

Source: First Steps in Starting a Foundation

     © *2006, Council on Foundations, Inc.*

Historical Background

Legislative history shows that the public support test was developed to define private foundations so they could be more effectively regulated and to provide for enhanced deductibility of contributions to public charities. Throughout the development of the public support test, it was apparent that Congress and the IRS believed that public support translates into more public oversight and accountability. As Thomas A. Troyer writes in *The 1969 Private Foundation Law: Historical Perspective on Its Origins and Underpinnings*, the theory was that if publicly supported organizations and other public charities "depended for their financial support on public or governmental contributors, at least some contributors of substantial amounts could be expected to have sufficient interest in the charities' affairs to look into what they were doing. The boards of such organizations were ordinarily composed of at least several independent individuals, generally a number of them, and to attract public support they often included individuals with established reputations, known and respected by people interested in the fields of the organizations' charitable work."[10] Under this theory, organizations that qualify as publicly supported would not require significant government oversight as their contributors or patrons could be expected to monitor their compliance with organizational goals. In contrast, private foundations, which do not require contributions from the public, would be subject to more stringent government oversight.

Although the concept of publicly supported charities appeared in the law earlier,[11] it was the Revenue Act of 1964 that finally began to define "publicly supported." Specifically, the act defined a publicly supported organization as one that normally received substantial support from governmental units or from the general public (directly or indirectly).[12] This definition was added for the purpose of permitting individuals to receive higher deductibility of charitable contributions to these publicly supported organizations. The full public support test discussed throughout this book was developed in regulations promulgated by the Treasury Department in 1973.[13]

Although much time has elapsed since the creation of the public support test, calculating the test is an ongoing challenge for publicly supported charities, especially community foundations. Young organizations become concerned that an unusually large contribution from one source might cause them to be reclassified as a private foundation. Older organizations discover the irony that the more successful the organization is at building its endowment, the more trouble it may have in meeting its public support test. This paradox is felt particularly acutely by community foundations; fulfilling the community foundation's purpose of developing a permanent endowment for the geographical area it serves makes it more difficult to pass the public support test because endowment income does not count as public support. Regardless of an organization's age or situation, understanding the public support test is essential to help a charity stay on course to maintain its status as a public charity.

---

[10] Washington, DC: Council on Foundations, 2000, p. 25.

[11] For a more in-depth historical picture of the development of the public support test and other aspects of charity governance, see Marion R. Fremont-Smith, *Governing Nonprofit Organizations: Federal and State Law and Regulation* (Cambridge: The Belknap Press of Harvard University Press, 2004).

[12] See Revenue Act of 1964, Pub. L. No. 88-272, § 209(a), 78 Stat 1134 (1964).

[13] See T.D. 7242 (1973-1 C.B. 118).

CHAPTER ONE

The Public Support Test: A General Explanation

Although the public support test may not be intuitive, it is understandable if broken down into its parts. This section will provide an overview of the test to show how all of the parts fit together.

The goal of the public support test is to demonstrate that the organization receives enough public support to qualify as a public charity instead of a private foundation. Described another way, the key element of this test is to show that a significant amount of the support generated by the public charity does not derive from just one person, one family or one company (as is the case with most private foundations). In short, publicly supported organizations must demonstrate a steady stream of contributions from a number of sources.

Components of the Public Support Test

A publicly supported organization demonstrates that it has the necessary amount of support by showing that normally a substantial part of its total support qualifies as public support. Each of these terms— "normally," "substantial," "total support" and "public support"—has a specific definition that will be parsed out in subsequent chapters.

Chapter 2 will examine what makes up the total support that a charity receives. In Chapter 3, the discussion will focus on what portions of total support will count as public support. Chapter 4 will review income excluded from both total support and public support. Chapter 5 will cover the time period over which the public support assessment is made and the length of time that publicly supported status lasts. Chapter 6 discusses the alternative test that may be applied.

Over and over again, you will see that there are many ways in which the Tax Code tries to make passing the public support test possible. For example, charities have a rolling period of four years to demonstrate that they meet the test. Charities that cannot meet the strictest form of the test—the mechanical test—have the option of meeting a flexible "facts and circumstances" test. Finally, new organizations typically have up to five years to develop their public support before proving that they meet the public support test.

Public Support Fraction

The heart of the public support test is determining the degree to which an organization is publicly supported. This determination is made, in many cases, simply by examining the percentage of public support the organization receives.

Because the amount of public support is expressed as a percentage, the key tool used to calculate the public support test is the "public support fraction." This fraction shows the ratio of public support to total support. At minimum, the percentage of public support must be 10 percent. A charity that obtains a

---

The Public Support Fraction

$$\frac{\text{Public Support}}{\text{Total Support}} = \frac{\text{Percentage}}{\text{of Public Support}}$$

---

public support percentage of 33 $1/3$ percent or more benefits from not having to document the facts and circumstances it relies upon to support the charity's classification as a publicly supported charity. (Chapter 6 provides more information about the required percentages.)

Throughout this book you will be referred back to this fraction to demonstrate where a particular piece of information fits into the analysis of whether an organization is publicly supported.

Accounting Method

Although there is no authoritative guidance on the subject of what accounting method must be used when calculating public support under Section 509(a)(1),[14] less formal guidance suggests the IRS position that organizations should report on a cash basis.[15]

Oversight

How can others—including the IRS—determine if an organization is meeting the public support test? Annually, an organization calculates and reports its public support on its Form 990, Schedule A[16] which is submitted to the IRS; a copy of this schedule is reproduced in Appendix D. Form 990 (including Schedule A) is the information return filed by Section 501(c)(3) public charities and other tax-exempt organizations. Form 990 is also publicly available through some organizations on the Internet as well as subject to mandatory disclosure requirements when the document is requested in person or in writing.[17] Although organizations normally receiving less than $25,000 annually in gross receipts are not required to file Form 990, these organizations should maintain records documenting the organizations' public support so this information can be provided in the event of an audit.[18]

---

[14] Note that for organizations operating under § 509(a)(2), Treas. Reg. § 1.509(a)-3(k) requires the use of the cash method of accounting.

[15] See G.C.M. 39109 (Jan. 20, 1982), which concludes that although the possibility of someone abusing the accrual method of accounting for purposes of calculating the public support test was remote, the regulations with regard to accounting method should be consistent between §§ 170(b)(1)(A)(vi) and 509(a)(2) of the Tax Code. Similarly, instructions for completing the public support schedule on Form 990, Schedule A note that the cash method of accounting should be used when completing the support schedule.

[16] Current forms and instructions can be found at www.irs.gov.

[17] For more information on the public disclosure rules, see IRS Publication 4221, *Compliance Guide for 501(c)(3) Tax-Exempt Organizations* (available at www.irs.gov).

[18] Although these organizations are not required to file Form 990, the Pension Protection Act of 2006 requires these organizations to provide certain basic information about the organization to the IRS on an annual basis. This provision is effective for annual periods which begin after 2006.

"Gross receipts" in this context is defined differently than the term is defined for the purposes of the public support test. In determining whether or not a public charity must file Form 990, gross receipts includes the total amount received from *all* sources without subtracting costs or expenses. "Normally" is also defined differently. Normally, in this context, is defined as averaging $25,000 or less in gross receipts for the three previous tax years. See *Instructions for Form 990 and Form 990-EZ* (available at www.irs.gov).

An organization that cannot show that it meets the public support test on its Form 990, Schedule A or otherwise will not lose its tax-exempt status but, instead, is subject to reclassification by the IRS as a private foundation. Chapter 8 discusses the consequences of failing the public support test.

Although the details and nuances of the public support test cannot be captured in any one chart, Figure 2 provides a shorthand reference to the elements of the public support test. Each of these elements will be explored in subsequent chapters. A chart of the elements of the public support test is also included in Appendix A.

Public Support: The Numerator	
1. Gifts, grants from private donors (persons, private foundations, bequests and corporations).	Included for each donor up to 2 percent of total support and may not include payments that qualify as gross receipts.*
2. Gifts, grants from public donors (governmental agencies or certain other publicly supported charities).	Included in full unless earmarked by original donor, in which case the 2 percent limitation applies (excluded if payment qualifies as gross receipt*).
3. Membership fees.	Included if basic purpose is general support.
4. Tax revenues levied on behalf of the organization.	Included.
5. Government services or facilities given without charge.	Included.

Total Support: The Denominator	
1. Gifts, grants from private donors (persons, private foundations, bequests and corporations).	Included in full, but may not include payments that qualify as gross receipts.*
2. Gifts, grants from public donors (governmental agencies or certain other publicly supported charities).	Included in full, but may not include payments that qualify as gross receipts.*
3. Membership fees.	Included if basic purpose is general support.
4. Tax revenues levied on behalf of that organization.	Included.
5. Government services or facilities given without charge.	Included.
6. Gross investment income.	Included.
7. Net unrelated business income.	Included.

Excluded from Support Fraction
1. Gross receipts income,* including membership fees or government grants that are for services and income from some fundraising events.
2. Unusual grants.
3. Voluntary services.
4. Capital gains, whether realized or unrealized.

* "Gross receipts income" is defined and discussed in Chapters 4 and 7.

CHAPTER TWO

Total Support: The Denominator

A publicly supported organization demonstrates that it has the necessary amount of support by showing that normally a substantial part of its *total support* qualifies as public support.

This chapter, will explore what kinds of contributions are—and are not— included in the total support number.

In calculating an organization's percentage of public support, it is easiest to first examine an organization's total support, the amount that is includible in the denominator of the public support fraction. In part, this is because what is includible as public support in the numerator of the fraction is a subset of total support.

Not all income a charity receives is included in total support; Chapter 4 identifies those types of income that are excluded. Below are the sources of support that must be included in the denominator as part of total support.[19]

Gifts, grants and contributions from individual donors, private foundations, corporations, bequests, other public charities or from other non-charitable tax-exempt organizations (for example, business leagues or chambers of commerce).[20] These can be direct contributions received from the original donor or indirect contributions received from an organization such as the United Way.

The Public Support Fraction		
$\dfrac{\text{Public Support}}{\text{Total Support}}$	=	Percentage of Public Support

Government grants or contracts as long as the purpose of the payment is primarily to enable the organization to provide a service to (or maintain a facility for) the direct benefit of the public.[21] For example, a grant from a government entity to a community foundation to make environmental grants with funds collected as fines for violations of environmental laws would clearly provide a service of direct benefit to the public. On the other hand, a contract to provide services to the government would not be includible in total support because the income would be payment for the performance of the organization's charitable

---

[19] Treas. Reg. § 1.170A-9(e)(7)(i).

[20] Treas. Reg. § 1.170A-9(e)(6)(i).

[21] Treas. Reg. § 1.170A-9(e)(8).

purpose. For example, payment under a contract from a state endowment for the arts to a community foundation to provide training to the state staff in setting up a grant review process would be excluded from total support. (See the discussions of gross receipts income in Chapters 4 and 7 for more information.)

Membership fees, if the basic purpose for paying such a fee is to provide general support for the organization.[22] If the purpose of the membership fee is to purchase admissions, merchandise or services, the membership fee could not be included in total support. (See the discussions of gross receipts income in Chapters 4 and 7 for more information.)

All net income from unrelated business activities whether or not such activities are carried on regularly as a trade or business. Unrelated business income is income generated from the operation of a trade or business—activity carried on for the production of income from selling goods or performing services—that is regularly carried on and not substantially related to the exempt purpose of the organization.[23]

Unrelated business income tax is the tax imposed on the income from such activities. A common way for charities to avoid the unrelated business income tax (UBIT) is to demonstrate that the activity is not regularly carried on, such as an occasional bake sale. Here, however, all unrelated business income (after subtracting appropriate expenses) counts as part of total support, **even if** the activity is not regularly carried on. Therefore, although net income from the occasional bake sale is not unrelated business income subject to tax, the proceeds will count as part of total support. Chapter 7 contains a more detailed discussion of this issue in the context of fundraising.

Gross investment income including interest, dividends, rent and royalties. One important exception: the realized gain from the sale of appreciated property is *not* included as part of gross investment income. Capital gains generated from the sale of appreciated property are not included in the public support fraction.

Tax revenues levied by a governmental unit for the benefit of the organization and either paid to it or expended on its behalf.

The value of services or facilities (exclusive of services or facilities generally furnished to the public without charge) provided by a governmental unit to the organization without charge. For example, if the local government provides free office space to the charity, the fair market value of the office space would be included in total support. Where the government provides something to the organization beyond what it provides to others, the value of the contribution counts in total support. However, such service or facility does *not* count as support if it is also provided for free to the public generally. In such a case it is excluded from the public support fraction.

All sources of income noted above count as total support. The key question is how much of it will also count as public support? Not all of it will.

---

[22]   Treas. Reg. § 1.170A-9(e)(7)(iii).

[23]   I.R.C. § 512. There are some exceptions to this definition. For example, investment income, royalties and some rental income is excluded.

CHAPTER THREE

Public Support: The Numerator

A publicly supported organization demonstrates that it has the necessary amount of support by showing that normally a substantial part of its total support qualifies as *public support.*

This chapter will describe which elements of total support count as public support.

As one works through the public support test calculation, it can be easy to lose sight of the test's purpose. Keeping in mind that the purpose of the public support test is to assess whether a charity has ongoing broad-based support helps to explain the limits on the type of income that counts as "public support."

The Public Support Fraction

$$\frac{\text{Public Support}}{\text{Total Support}} = \text{Percentage of Public Support}$$

A good rule to remember is that all income that counts as public support also counts as part of total support, but not all total support counts as public support (Figure 3). Below are the only sources of support that may count as public support in the numerator of the public support fraction.

FIGURE 3: COMPARING TYPES OF SUPPORT

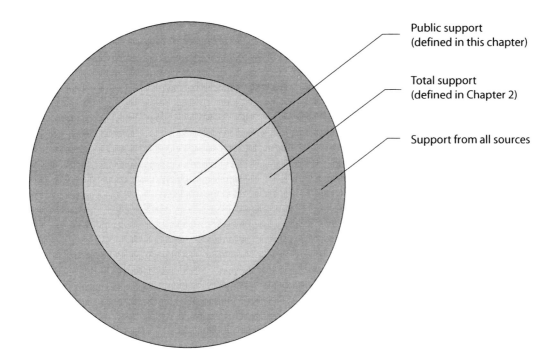

Public support
(defined in this chapter)

Total support
(defined in Chapter 2)

Support from all sources

Gifts, grants and contributions from individual donors, private foundations, corporations, bequests or other non-charitable tax-exempt organizations. However, contributions from these donors are not 100 percent includible as public support.

When determining public support, each donor's contributions are limited to an amount equal to or less than *2 percent* of the charity's total support.[24] For example: if total support for the four-year period is $100,000, contributions from one donor of $40,000 during the four-year period will all count as total support, but only $2,000 (2 percent of $100,000) will count as public support. (See Chapter 5 for a discussion of the four-year period.) This limitation applies even if the donor is a corporation or organization. (See the sidebar on page 9 to learn when donors' contributions must be aggregated for the purposes of determining the amount includible in public support.)

---

24 Treas. Reg. § 1.170A-9(e)(6)(i).

The 2 Percent Limitation

The policy behind the public support test for public charities is to ensure that these organizations have broad sources of support; the 2 percent limitation is a necessary (albeit complicated) way of preventing abuse. Essentially the 2 percent limitation ensures that a charity will have to seek support from multiple individuals, corporations and foundations. Here's a simple formulation of the rule: No matter how much one of these donors contributes to a public charity, no more than an amount equal to 2 percent of the charity's total support (the denominator) can count as public support (the numerator). The entire contribution must be considered part of total support.

Typically, the limitation on the inclusion of contributions from individuals, corporations and organizations as public support is calculated based on the identity of the donor; each donor's contributions are aggregated during the relevant four-year period.

> *Example: Total support during the four-year period is $200,000. Two percent of the total support is $4,000. The charity could only include up to $4,000 of each individual's contribution in public support regardless of the amount above $4,000 each individual actually contributed over the four-year period.*

Sometimes contributions must be aggregated before calculating the portion of the contribution that is includible as public support. The rationale for this aggregation is to ensure that the charity is supported by a variety of sources and not just one or a few family members and/or related corporations.

All contributions made by a donor and by any other person or persons listed below shall be treated as coming from the donor and thus aggregated:

- The donor's spouse, ancestors, children, grandchildren, great-grandchildren and the spouses of children, grandchildren and great-grandchildren.

- A corporation, partnership or trust if such an entity is a substantial contributor to the organization and the donor owns more than 20 percent of the voting power, profits interest or beneficial interest of the entity.

There are other relationships involving corporations, partnerships and trusts in which the 2 percent limitation may also apply. The other relationships are described in I.R.C. Section 4946(a)(1)(C)-(G). Because of their complexity, such relationships are not provided here, but for situations in which donors have significant rights or ownership interests involving corporations, partnerships and trusts that also contribute to the organization, legal consultation is strongly advised.

Gifts or grants from other public charities count as public support and are not subject to the 2 percent limitation when they are from other charities classified as public charities under Sections 509(a)(1) and 170(b)(1)(A)(vi).[25] This is true whether contributed directly or indirectly. For example, 100 percent of a grant from a United Way or a grant from a donor-advised fund held by a community foundation would normally count as public support. In the rarer occasion that the funds from the publicly supported charity originally came from an individual donor (person, private foundation or corporation) and were "earmarked" for the ultimate recipient, the contribution would be subject to the 2 percent limitation. (See the sidebar for more information about earmarking.)

Although the Treasury regulations themselves state only that contributions from other Section 170(b)(1)(A)(vi) charities are not subject to the 2 percent limitation, subsequent IRS guidance suggests that contributions from other Section 509(a)(1) organizations such as churches, schools and medical institutions should not be subject to the 2 percent limitation, if, in fact, the church, school or medical institution is actually publicly supported and could meet the public support test discussed in this publication.[26]

Two Percent Limitation	
Public Charity Classification	**Subject to 2% Limitation?**
§§ 509(a)(1) and 170(b)(1)(A)(vi)—Publicly supported organization	No
§§ 509(a)(1) and 170(b)(1)(A)(i)-(v)—Churches, schools, etc.	No—If organization could meet the public support test under § 170(b)(1)(A)(vi)
§ 509(a)(2)—Gross Receipts Organization	Yes
§ 509(a)(3)—Supporting Organization	Yes

Contributions from public charities recognized under Section 509(a)(2) that receive income through sales of merchandise, admissions or other income raised through the performance of their exempt purpose are subject to the 2 percent limitation.

Supporting organizations are public charities under Section 509(a)(3) that are categorized as such because of their relationship with one or more publicly supported organizations. Supporting organizations are not publicly supported themselves. For this reason, contributions from supporting organizations are subject to the 2 percent limitation.

Because of the different treatment of contributions from the different types of public charities, the recipient organization will need to determine the status of the contributing public charity. This can often be most readily handled by requesting a copy of the donor's IRS determination letter, which often contains the needed information.

Government grants or contracts that are includible in total support are also includible in public support. Income of this type from governmental units is not subject to the 2 percent limitation—100 percent of such support counts as public.[27]

---

[25]   Treas. Reg. § 1.170-9(e)(6)(v).

[26]   Virginia G. Richardson and John Francis Reilly, "Public Charity or Private Foundation Status Issues under IRC 509(a)(1)-(4), 4942(j)(3), and 507" in IRS *Exempt Organization-Technical Instruction Program for FY 2003*, (hereinafter "Public Charity or Private Foundation"), p. B-57, available at http://www.irs.gov/pub/irs-tege/eotopicb03.pdf. See also Rev. Rul. 78-95, 1978-C.B. 71.

[27]   Treas. Reg. § 1.170A-9(e)(6)(i).

Membership fees, tax revenues and the value of services or facilities includible in total support are also entirely includible in public support. (See Chapter 2 for more information.)

By contrast, the following sources of total support *do not* count as public support: (1) portions of gifts or grants from individual donors (persons, private foundations or corporations) that are excluded because of the 2 percent limitation; (2) gross investment income; and (3) net unrelated business income, whether the business is carried on regularly or not.

Treatment of Earmarked Gifts or Grants

In most cases, gifts from governmental units or other publicly supported organizations are not subject to the 2 percent limitation. In theory, gifts from government or publicly supported organizations by definition are not from one person, one family or one corporation. As noted above, however, if the original donor attempts to funnel a gift through the governmental unit or publicly supported charity to get around this rule, the regulations will treat the gift as made directly by the original donor, subject to the 2 percent limitation, if the original grant is implicitly or expressly earmarked. An earmarked gift is generally defined as one that is subject to an oral or written agreement requiring the intermediary donee agency to convey the gift to a subsequent donee.

Special Issues for Community Foundations: Treatment of Contributions to and from Funds at a Community Foundation

Community foundations are organized to hold a variety of funds, including donor-advised funds, designated funds and agency endowments.[28] These funds present special issues affecting the application of the public support test because these funds include elements of ongoing advice from donors, in the case of donor-advised funds, or donor restrictions on permissible grants from the fund, in the case of designated funds and agency endowments. For community foundations, the key question is whether the contributions to these types of funds held by a community foundation are considered public support for the community foundation or for the organizations that ultimately receive grants from the funds. For public charities receiving grants from these funds, the central issue is whether the grants count as public support from the community foundation itself—counting as 100 percent public support—or as an indirect contribution earmarked from the initial donor.

The critical factor in both of these determinations is whether the contribution to a community foundation for one of these funds is subject to the discretion and control of the community foundation or is an "earmarked" contribution. A contribution subject to the discretion and control of the community foundation should likely count as public support for the community foundation and should receive the most favorable treatment when granted to another Section 501(c)(3) publicly supported charity. An earmarked contribution— a contribution subject to an oral or written understanding that it will be disbursed to a particular grantee—would unlikely count at all as public support for a community foundation. Similarly, an earmarked contribution would be unlikely to be considered support from a charity when paid out to a

---

28 For more information on these funds see Elaine Gast, *Community Foundation Handbook: What You Need to Know* (Council on Foundations, 2006).

© 2006, Council on Foundations, Inc.

grantee. Instead, it would be considered support from the donor and might be subject to the 2 percent limitation. A discussion of the likely treatment of contributions to and from various types of funds follows.

Donor-advised Funds

Donor-advised funds allow donors to recommend grants for charitable purposes. Contributions to donor-advised funds may be made by individuals, corporations or other charities. A key aspect of donor-advised funds is that a community foundation or other public charity that holds the donor-advised fund has the ultimate control over distributions. Thus, donors may *recommend* contributions from the fund, but they may not earmark contributions. Accordingly, the IRS has held in Private Letter Ruling 200037053 that donations to a donor-advised fund count as publicly supported for the purposes of the public support test.[29]

Similarly, contributions from donor-advised funds held by a community foundation to another public charity should be treated as public support from the community foundation and not from the donor-advisor. Because the funds are from a publicly supported charity, they are not subject to the 2 percent limitation when received by the public charity.[30]

Designated Funds and Agency Endowments

Designated funds and agency endowments are established at a community foundation to benefit a specific charity. The difference is that designated funds are established with contributions from individuals or others for the benefit of a charity (or charities). The donor makes the designation at the time of the gift and may not change the recipient after the gift is made. An agency endowment is a fund established by a public charity at a community foundation to benefit itself. In this case the public charity is both donor and recipient. In both of these cases, the community foundation retains the power to shift distributions away from the designated agency should the community foundation deem it advisable (this power is often referred to as the variance power).[31] Although this power is rarely exercised, its existence is enough to demonstrate the community foundation's discretion and control over the donated funds. Because the com-

---

[29] Although private letter rulings may not be relied upon by organizations other than those that requested the ruling, private letter rulings do provide some indication of the IRS's thinking on a particular topic.

[30] In a case where substantially all of a recipient charity's support comes through a donor-advised fund, the IRS could argue that the contributions from the donor-advised fund are, in actuality, from the original donor and not from the public charity and therefore could subject the contribution to the recipient charity to the 2 percent limitation. Whether or not such an argument would prevail in a case in which the contributions are not earmarked by the original donor is unknown.

[31] See Treas. Reg. § 1.170A-9(e)(11)(ii)(v)(B) providing that the governing body of a community trust must have the power "[t]o modify any restriction on condition on the distribution of funds for any specified charitable purposes or to specified organizations if in the sole judgment of the governing body (without the necessity of the approval of any participating trustee, custodian, or agent), such restriction or condition becomes, in effect, unnecessary, incapable of fulfillment, or inconsistent with the charitable needs of the community or area served."

munity foundation has discretion and control over the money, the funds are *not* earmarked for the agency. Thus, the contributions to an agency endowment or designated fund at a community foundation should count as public support.[32] Whether or not such a contribution is subject to the 2 percent limitation discussed above will depend on the identity of the donor. If the donor is a publicly supported charity the contribution would not be subject to the 2 percent limitation. If the contribution is from an individual or corporation, the amount included as public support would be affected by the 2 percent limitation.

Contributions from a designated fund should count as public support to the recipient charity as well. Once again, because the community foundation maintains discretion and control over the contributions, they are not "earmarked."

The key to deciding how to treat funds to or from an intermediary is summarized in a statement by the IRS in continuing professional education material for agents. It reads:

> [t]he substance of a transaction will always govern, and if the publicly supported organization or governmental unit is merely a conduit for amounts which have been expressly or impliedly earmarked by a donor as being for the particular organization, the contributions will be treated as having been made by the original donor and the 2 percent limitation will apply.[33]

Whether the fund is donor-advised, designated or an agency endowment, the IRS could look to the substance of the transaction, particularly in the event the intermediary public charity was being used in a manner to circumvent the 2 percent limitation contained in the public support test.

---

[32] In continuing professional education material the IRS has indicated that contributions to a community trust that qualify as component funds of the trust would be includible as public support to the community foundation. Presumably this reasoning would carry over to community foundations in the corporate form that follow the community trust rules by analogy. More recently, in addressing the question of whether a contribution to a donor-advised fund held by an intermediary public charity was public support to the intermediary, the IRS looked to the Treasury Regulations for termination of private foundations to determine the issue of whether the intermediary had dominion and control over the contribution to the donor-advised fund. The specific reference is to Treas. Reg. § 1.507-2(a)(8) which, in part, states that a charity has dominion and control over a contribution to a designated fund as long as the recipient names the designated charity at the time of the gift and not subsequent to the gift.

   What if the intermediary charity does not exercise discretion and control? Does money given to such a group for subsequent distribution to another charity count as public support? This is a question that could arise for donor-directed funds (i.e., funds where the donor reserves the right to direct contributions) or designated funds held by charities that do not follow the community trust rules, I.R.C. §170(b)(1)(E)(iii). The IRS has not provided clear guidance on this issue. One line of argument, presented by General Counsel Memorandum 37945 (August 3, 1988) seems to indicate that such a gift does count as public support for the intermediary grantee. In part, this opinion states "that earmarked contributions should be treated the same as non-earmarked contributions for purposes of determining the [public] support fraction...." The only exception to this rule discussed in the opinion is when the intermediary charity receives earmarked contributions "only as the agent of the donors for delivery to the ultimate recipients." However, the IRS specifically withdrew this General Counsel Memorandum by General Counsel Memorandum 39875 (June 28, 1995) so that the IRS could reconsider the issues involved. At this time, no additional guidance has been issued.

[33] Public Charity or Private Foundation, p. B-59.

CHAPTER FOUR

Income Excluded from Both Parts of the Support Fraction

A publicly supported organization demonstrates that it has the necessary amount of support by showing that normally a substantial part of its total support qualifies as public support. However, some support is disregarded for the purposes of the public support test.

This chapter will discuss income excluded from the numerator and the denominator of the public support fraction.

As noted previously, certain sources of support are excluded completely in calculating the public support fraction. Because the sources of income described below are not includible as public support or total support, they do not affect the charity's public support percentage. These sources are:

A. **Voluntary services.** Contributions of services for which a charitable deduction is not allowable do not count as either public support or total support.[34] An individual taxpayer may not deduct the value of voluntary time given to charity. Thus, the value of the time provided by an attorney, an accountant or a loaned executive from a business corporation is not deductible by the donor (or the corporation that employs the worker) and is excluded completely in the calculation of the public support fraction.[35]

B. **Gross receipts income.** Any amount received by a charity that is, in effect, not a gift but a payment for the exercise or performance by the organization of its charitable purposes does not count as either public support or total support.[36] Examples of payments that would constitute gross receipts income are admission fees, merchandise sales, services performed or facilities. As noted in the introduction, charities that rely primarily on gross receipts income maintain their public status by meeting a different

---

[34] Treas. Reg. § 1.170A-9(e)(7)(i)(B).

[35] Other contributions that are not captured in the public support fraction include out-of-pocket expenses that individuals incur but do not report to the charity.

[36] Treas. Reg. § 1.170A-9(e)(7)(i)(A). Note that Treas. Reg. § 1.170A-9(e)(7)(ii) provides that if almost all of an organization's support is gross receipts income and an insignificant amount is from government or the public, the organization will not be classified as a § 170(b)(1)(A)(vi) organization. Such an organization would likely qualify as a public charity under § 509(a)(2).

public support test not discussed in this book.[37] If the basic purpose of a membership fee is to purchase admissions, merchandise or services, such a fee would constitute gross receipts income and be excluded from public support calculations.

Gross receipts income also includes income from certain fundraising events. Chapter 7 has a thorough discussion of accounting for fundraising events, including donor-initiated fundraising.

C. **Capital gains.** Whether realized (the appreciated property is sold) or unrealized (the appreciated property has gained in value but has not been sold), such gains are not included as public support or total support.[38] This may be particularly helpful if a charity sells a capital asset and incurs large capital gains in one year.

D. **Unusual grants.** The ability to treat an abnormally large gift or contribution as an unusual grant and thus exclude it from the public support test calculations can be very beneficial to a community foundation or other charity.[39] Remember that 100 percent of a grant counts as total support (in the denominator), but only a small portion of such grants can usually count as public support (in the numerator) because of the 2 percent limitation rule noted earlier. The determination of whether a grant or other contribution qualifies as an "unusual grant" is based upon a variety of factors.[40] In simplified terms, a substantial contribution or bequest will qualify as an unusual grant if it satisfies three conditions. The gift must:

1. Be attracted by reason of the publicly supported nature of the organization.

2. Be unusual or unexpected with respect to the amount.

3. By reason of its size, adversely affect the public charity status of the organization (in other words, tip it into private foundations status by making it fail the public support test—see discussion of "tipping" in Chapter 8 and Appendix B).

---

[37] See Internal Revenue Code §509(a)(2) and related regulations.

[38] If the capital asset is debt-financed such that the gains are subject to unrelated business income tax, capital gains would be includible in total support but not public support because the gains would be considered unrelated business income.

[39] See Treas. Reg. §1.170A-9(e)(6)(ii); Rev. Proc. 81-6, 1981-1 C.B. 620; and Rev. Proc. 81-7, 1981-1 C.B. 621.

[40] See Treas. Reg. §1.170A-9(e)(6)(ii); Rev. Proc. 81-6, 1981-1 C.B. 620; and Rev. Proc. 81-7, 1981-1 C.B. 621. Rev. Proc. 81-7 is reproduced in Appendix C.

The IRS considers other factors in determining whether a grant qualifies as an unusual grant. The examination focuses on both the contribution itself as well as the activities of the charity before receiving the gift. Among the factors the IRS considers favorable in determining if a grant is an unusual grant are whether:

1. The contribution was made by a person not connected to the charity, i.e., not a former board member or substantial contributor to the foundation.

2. The contribution was a bequest.

3. The contribution was in cash, readily marketable securities or assets that further the exempt purpose of an organization.

4. The gift was free of any material restrictions.

5. The charity met the mechanical test in previous years without any grants classified as unusual.

6. The charity's governing body is broadly based.[41]

Unusual grants do not necessarily require an advance ruling from the IRS, but when such a gift is anticipated, a ruling is often advisable to protect both the donor and the public charity. Retaining experienced legal counsel is recommended when unusual grants are at issue.

E. Interfund transfers. Funds transferred within a public charity do not count as total or public support. For example, fees taken by community foundations from individual component funds to support the general operation of the charity are interfund transfers. Such fees are entirely excluded from the calculation of the public support fraction because the fees are not new contributions to the community foundation. Instead, these fees represent accounting transfers from one fund to another.

---

[41] Public Charity or Private Foundation, p. B-50.

CHAPTER FIVE

Normally: Defining the Period of Time

A publicly supported organization demonstrates that it has the necessary amount of support by showing that *normally* a substantial part of its total support qualifies as public support.

This chapter addresses the questions: What period of time does the IRS consider to determine whether a charity is publicly supported? How long does publicly supported status last?

Although many public charity managers presume that their organizations must meet the public support test each tax year based solely on contributions from that tax year, the IRS has defined "normally" quite differently. The Treasury regulations actually define normally to mean over a *four-year period*.[42] In other words, to meet the public support test the organization must demonstrate that, during the applicable four-year rolling period, a substantial part of its total support is public support. The result of defining normally to mean over a four-year period is that rules are fairly lenient: one year of very poor public support will not threaten the public status of the organization if sufficient public support is obtained before and after that year.

Determining the Four-Year Period

Support from the current tax year is not included when calculating an organization's percentage of public support. Instead, the calculation is based entirely on the four previous tax years.[43] For example, to determine whether a public charity has satisfied the public support test for 2006, the years that are included in the calculation are 2005, 2004, 2003 and 2002. Support during 2006—the current year—is irrelevant as to whether or not the community foundation is publicly supported during 2006.

---

[42] Treas. Reg. § 1.170A-9(e)(4).

[43] The current year's Support Schedule on Part IV-A of Form 990, Schedule A will specifically outline which four years should be included in the calculation.

The Grace Year

If a public charity passes the public support test for the current tax year, the IRS actually treats the charity as publicly supported for two years: the current tax year *and* the subsequent tax year.[44] For example, if a community foundation has passed the support test for its current year (2006) by computing support from 2005, 2004, 2003 and 2002, then it will be considered publicly supported for the current year (2006) *and the next year* (2007). This treatment is another way in which the public support test is more lenient than one may initially believe.

Five-Year Measuring Period Exception

Under fairly rare circumstances outlined in Treas. Reg. § 1.170A-9(e)(4)(v), the IRS will apply a five-year period that includes the four previous years (as above) plus the current tax year. Specifically, this exception only applies if there is a "substantial and material" change in the organization's sources of support during the current tax year. An example of such a change could be an unusually large contribution or bequest that does not qualify as an unusual grant. (Unusual grants are described more in detail in Chapter 4, but are generally grants that are attracted because of the publicly supported nature of the organization, are unusual or unexpected, and would adversely affect the organization's public charity status. If an organization can demonstrate that a large gift is an unusual grant it can have the gift excluded from its public support calculation.) Thus, in a year during which a public charity has met the public support test based on the four previous years, a very large grant (that fails to qualify as an unusual grant) in the current year may cause the organization to lose its public charity status if the IRS applies this optional five-year computation period. Unfortunately, the IRS has not provided additional guidance as to when they will use this five-year standard.

---

44 Treas. Reg. § 1.170A-9(e)(4).

Demonstrating the Flexibility of the Public Support Test

The flexibility of this public support test is further illustrated by closer examination of how the rules above actually work in practice. This is best explained in an example that assumes there are no "substantial and material" changes occurring during the period in question, a circumstance that would permit the IRS to use a five-year computation period. In this example, County Community Foundation is a publicly supported organization with a calendar tax year.

STEP 1: County Community Foundation has a bad year in 2005 in generating public support. Yet, in early 2006 when it files its 2005 tax return, it can demonstrate that it has passed the public support test using the appropriate four-year period for the calculations, namely, the previous four tax years *which do not include* 2005 (2004 + 2003 + 2002 + 2001). As a result, the foundation is considered to be publicly supported for 2005 (the year for which it is filing its tax return) and 2006 (the immediately succeeding tax year). However, County Community Foundation knows it will be in trouble soon unless it makes good use of its "grace year" (2006) and brings in substantial public support.

STEP 2: In early 2007, when it is time to file its tax return for the 2006 tax year, County Community Foundation will have to include the bad year (2005) in its public support test calculations. It will fail both the mechanical test (one-third) and the facts and circumstances test (10 percent) using the appropriate four-year period for the calculations, namely, the previous four tax years (2005 + 2004 + 2003 + 2002). (See Chapter 6 for more information about these two tests.) Is it publicly supported for the tax year for which it is filing a return (2006)? Yes, because it qualified for two years under STEP 1 and one of those years was 2006. However, at this point, the tax return that will have to be filed for tax year 2007 is not protected by the grace period.

STEP 3: Recognizing the problems created by the bad year in 2005, County Community Foundation makes an extra effort in 2006 (its grace year) to bring in solid public support and is successful. Thus, when it files its 2007 tax return, County Community Foundation will again, because of its 2006 efforts, pass the public support test using the appropriate four-year period for the calculations, namely, the previous four tax years (2006-good year + 2005-bad year + 2004 + 2003).

In summary, despite filing a 2006 tax return showing that it had failed the public support test for the applicable four-year period, County Community Foundation maintains its public charity status for all applicable years.

Defining "Normally" for New Organizations

If an organization has existed for at least eight months, but for fewer than five taxable years, the four-year computation period will not apply. Instead, the IRS will apply the test to the number of years the organization has existed immediately preceding the current taxable year. For example, if the current taxable year is 2006, and the organization was created on January 1, 2004, the computation period will consist of two years: 2004 + 2005.

In lieu of using the modified period of time described above, many new publicly supported charities request an "advance ruling" regarding their public charity status. (Organizations that have not been in existence for at least eight months are required to request an advance ruling.) This advance ruling period allows the new charity to be recognized by the IRS as a publicly supported charity for a period of five years (beginning with the organization's first tax year) before it must prove that it meets the public support test.[45] Within 90 days of the end of this five-year period, the organization is required to demonstrate that it has met the public support test using the full five-year advance period as its base of calculations. IRS Form 8734, Support Schedule for Advance Ruling Period is the document that public charities nearing the end of their advance ruling period must complete.[46] The form is very similar to the public support schedule contained in the Form 990, Schedule A although it requests information for a five-year period of time. The advance ruling period is beneficial to most charities because it allows them to develop a broader donor base than they often are able to achieve immediately upon formation.

Importance of Promptly Obtaining a Final Determination

So that donors may rely on an organization's tax determination letter, any publicly supported charity with an advance ruling letter must—within 90 days after its advance period ending—submit to the IRS adequate documentation that it has met the public support test during the advance ruling period and request a final tax determination ruling. Failure to request a final ruling by filing for IRS Form 8734 in a timely manner may prompt the IRS to consider reclassification of the organization to private foundation status.

The other potential hazard of not being attentive to the expiration of the organization's advance ruling is that funders are reluctant to make grants to an organization with an expired advance ruling and no permanent ruling letter. If the charity is within the 90-day period after the expiration of the advance ruling period, a grantor is likely to request a copy of the documentation (Form 8734) the potential grantee submitted to the IRS and any subsequent correspondence with the IRS. If the charity is outside the 90-day period, a private foundation will likely choose to treat the grant as a grant to a noncharity to avoid any risk that the IRS will impose penalties on the private foundation; such treatment will require the private foundation to exercise extra due diligence through a process called expenditure responsibility. While some private foundations may be willing to take these extra steps, others may choose to wait until the potential grantee receives clarification of its status from the IRS.

---

[45] If the IRS deems the organization eligible for a charitable tax exemption, the new charity's determination letter will provide a specific date when the advance ruling expires. Although Treas. Reg. § 1.170A-9(e)(5)(i) provides for an advance ruling period of two or three years, the IRS uses a five-year advance ruling period. This change is reflected in IRS forms and publications, but the Treasury regulations have not been revised to reflect the change.

Organizations requesting an advance ruling period are required to consent to extend the statue of limitations period for actions within the five tax years during the extension for a period of eight years, four months and 15 days after the first tax year. The consent is now incorporated into IRS Form 1023, *Application for Recognition of Exemption Under Section 501(c)(3) of the Internal Revenue Code*. If the organization does not qualify as a public charity at the end of the advance ruling period, the IRS can impose private foundation excise taxes for the advance ruling period.

[46] Form 8734 may be downloaded from the IRS website at www.irs.gov.

CHAPTER SIX

Substantial: How Much Public Support Is Enough?

A publicly supported organization demonstrates that it has the necessary amount of support by showing that normally a *substantial* part of its total support qualifies as public support.

This chapter will discuss income excluded from the numerator and the denominator of the public support fraction.

Publicly supported charities must show that a substantial part of their total support is public support. The IRS has quantified "substantial" as a percentage. While previous chapters define "total support" and "public support," this chapter numerically defines the goal of the calculation. At minimum, at least 10 percent of an organization's total support must be public support. However, unless one-third (or $33^1/3$ percent) of a charity's percentage of total support is public support, the charity will have to document the facts and circumstances that buttress the charity's classification as publicly supported. These rules are encapsulated in two tests: the mechanical test and the facts and circumstances test.

Mechanical Test

Charities may show that they have a substantial amount of public support by meeting the mechanical test. This test is called the "mechanical test" because it relies simply on a mathematical formula. If, during the relevant period of calculation, the amount of public support equals or exceeds **one-third** (or $33^1/3$

The Public Support Fraction
$\dfrac{\text{Public Support}}{\text{Total Support}}$ = Percentage of Public Support

percent) of total eligible support, the organization has passed the mechanical test and will continue to qualify as a public charity.[47] Specifically, to pass the mechanical test, public support—the amount above the line of the fraction (the numerator)—must equal or exceed one-third of total support—the amount below the line (the denominator).

---

[47] Treas. Reg. § 1.170A-9(e)(2).

Facts and Circumstances Test

If the organization fails to pass the mechanical test, there is still a second chance (or fallback test) to show that the charity is publicly supported; this second test is known as the "facts and circumstances test." Thus, even though the percentage of public support falls below one-third, the organization may still qualify as a public charity, depending on all the facts and circumstances.[48] To qualify under this fallback test, the organization *must* be able to demonstrate two elements:

1. The total amount of public support must equal or exceed an *absolute minimum of 10 percent* of total support for the applicable period.[49] An organization that does not obtain 10 percent of public support risks being reclassified as a private foundation.

2. The organization must be organized and operated to attract new and additional public support on a continuous basis. Treasury regulations state that "[a]n organization will be considered to meet this requirement if it maintains a continuous and bona fide program for solicitation of funds from the general public, community, or membership group involved…consideration will be given to whether the scope of its fund-raising activities is reasonable in light of its charitable activities."[50]

In addition to meeting both of the above requirements, all pertinent facts and circumstances surrounding the operations of the organization will be taken into consideration in determining whether this test is sufficiently satisfied. The Treasury regulations list five facts and circumstances that will be considered as important factors.[51] An organization is not required to satisfy all of the factors, nor are the five factors listed exclusive—others may reasonably be considered such as the purpose of the organization and the length of time the organization has existed.

Factors

1. *Percentage of financial support.*[52] The higher the percentage of public support *above* the minimum 10 percent requirement, the lesser will be the burden of establishing the publicly supported nature of the organization through other factors. Obviously, the converse is also true. If the percentage of public support barely exceeds the minimum (11 percent, for example), other facts and circumstances will need to be present that strongly suggest the public nature of the organization.

2. *Sources of support.*[53] The issue raised by this factor is: How broad is the base of support? Is the support from governmental units and a "representative number of persons," or is most of the support from the members of a single family? The Treasury regulations make clear that in determining what constitutes a representative number of persons, consideration will be given to "the

---

[48] Treas. Reg. § 1.170A-9(e)(3).

[49] Treas. Reg. § 1.170A-9(e)(3)(i).

[50] Treas. Reg. §170A-9(e)(3)(ii). The regulations governing the treatment of community trusts also acknowledge the special nature of community trusts. The regulations expressly indicate that community trusts are not required to engage in periodic, communitywide fundraising campaigns aimed at attracting a large number of small contributions to meet the facts and circumstances test. Instead, these regulations specifically state that community trusts will generally satisfy the element of attraction of public support if "they seek gifts and bequests from a wide range of potential donors in the community or area served, through banks or trust companies, through attorneys or other professional persons, or in other appropriate ways which call attention to the community trust as a potential recipient of gifts and bequests made for the benefit of the community or area served." Treas. Reg. §1.170A-9(e)(10).

[51] Treas. Reg. § 1.170A-9(e)(3)(ii).

[52] Treas. Reg. § 1.170A-9(e)(3)(iii).

[53] Treas. Reg. § 1.170A-9(e)(3)(iv).

type of organization involved, the length of time it has been in existence, and whether it limits its activities to a particular community or region or to a special field which can be expected to appeal to a limited number of persons."[54]

3. *Representative governing body.*[55] Under this factor, an organization will benefit the more it can demonstrate that its governing body "represents the broad interest of the public, rather that the personal or private interests of a limited number of donors." Strict quotas are not required under this factor. The regulations make clear that a governing body will be deemed "representative" if it is composed "of public officials acting in their capacities as such; of individuals selected by public officials acting in their official capacities as such; of persons having special knowledge or expertise in the particular field or discipline in which the organization is operating; of community leaders, such as elected or appointed officials, clergy, educators, civic leaders, or other such persons representing a broad cross-section of the view and interests of the community."[56]

4. *Availability of public facilities or services; public participation in programs or policies.*[57] To the extent any charity can show that its facilities, programs, activities, services or policies are open to the public, used by the public or involve significant input from public officials or the public at large, this factor will be helpful in passing the facts and circumstances test. Museums, libraries and performing arts groups benefit most from this factor because their buildings and performances are open to the public. However, a community foundation may take advantage of this factor as well by continually offering services to donors in planning their giving and establishing funds.

5. *Factors pertinent to membership organizations.*[58] These factors include whether or not the dues rates and member solicitations are designed to attract membership from a broad cross-section of the public or a substantial number of persons in the community, particular profession or field of interest. Also examined are whether the activities of the organization are likely to appeal to persons having some broad common interest or purpose.

An organization receives the same IRS classification and benefits of a public charity organized under Sections 509(a)(1) and 170(b)(1)(A)(vi) regardless of whether or not the charity meets the public support test under the mechanical or the facts and circumstances test. In terms of reporting, all publicly supported charities complete the Support Schedule on Form 990, Schedule A, but organizations meeting the public support test under the facts and circumstances test should set forth the facts and circumstances upon which they base their conclusion in a statement that accompanies the form.[59]

---

[54] Id.

[55] Treas. Reg. § 1.170A-9(e)(3)(v).

[56] Treas. Reg. § 170A-9(e)(3)(v).

[57] Treas. Reg. § 1.170A-9(e)(3)(vi).

[58] Treas. Reg. § 1.170A-9(e)(3)(vii).

[59] *Instructions for Schedule A (Form 990 or 990-EZ)* (available at www.irs.gov).

The Public Support Test—A Hard Test to Fail

Although initially the public support test may seem difficult to pass, the reality is that it is unlikely that one gift will cause a charity to fail the public support test and be reclassified as a private foundation.

To illustrate just how hard it is to fail, consider the "rule of 8.76" and the "rule of 46." How large a gift or bequest will it take to "tip" the public charity—that is, to force it into private foundation status?

Assume that a publicly supported charity has been receiving a steady stream of small gifts adding up to roughly the same amount of support each year and that there is no other source of support. In such a case, it would take a gift more than 8.76 times the annual level of support to make the charity fail the mechanical (one-third) test, and a gift more than 46 times the annual level of support to make the charity fail the facts and circumstances (10 percent of support) test.

Illustration A. County Community Foundation for several years has received small gifts adding up to $100,000 annually. Suddenly, one new donor gives the community foundation $876,000. Does the community foundation still pass the mechanical test? YES.

TOTAL SUPPORT=

$876,000 + $400,000 (4 years x $100,000) = $1,276,000

PUBLIC SUPPORT =

$400,000 + $25,520 (2% of $1,276,000)= $425,520

$$\frac{\text{PUBLIC SUPPORT}}{\text{TOTAL SUPPORT}} = \frac{\$425,520}{\$1,276,000} = 33\%$$

Illustration B. Assume the same facts as illustration A, except the new donor makes a gift of $4.6 million. Does the community foundation still pass the facts and circumstances test? Yes, if it maintains an ongoing fundraising campaign and has good facts and circumstances.

TOTAL SUPPORT =

$4,600,000 + $400,000 (4 years • $100,000) = $5,000,000

PUBLIC SUPPORT =

$400,000 + $100,000 (2% of $5,000,000) = $ 500,000

$$\frac{\text{PUBLIC SUPPORT}}{\text{TOTAL SUPPORT}} = \frac{\$500,000}{\$5,000,000} = 10\%$$

Obviously, this is an oversimplified example that does not take into account many factors that are part of a typical charity's total and public support (it ignores gross investment income, for example). Nevertheless, the point is made: For a publicly supported organization with good facts and circumstances, it would take—relatively—an unusually large gift to make the charity fail the public support test.

CHAPTER SEVEN

Incorporating Fundraising Events in the Public Support Fraction

A publicly supported organization demonstrates that it has the necessary amount of support by showing that normally a substantial part of its total support qualifies as public support.

This chapter will review where to fit fundraising income into the public support fraction.

Community foundations and other public charities may raise money through events, such as dinners, auctions or golf tournaments, or by promising a donor an item in return for the contribution. Fundraising activities that generate contributions that are part charitable contribution and part payment for goods or services (e.g., a gift certificate or round of golf) must be accounted for differently than the typical charitable contribution. Additional issues arise when donors initiate fundraising activities either on their own or on behalf of the community foundation. The impact of both of these issues on the public support test is explored below.

A. **Disregarded benefits.** To be considered a "gift, grant or contribution" for the purposes of the public support test, a payment of money or transfer of property must be gratuitous; the donor may not receive benefits in return for the contribution. However, the IRS has determined that certain benefits are **disregarded** for the purposes of determining the amount of a contribution. When a donor only receives disregarded benefits, the entire amount of the donor's contribution is treated as a gift, grant or contribution for the purposes of public support. Disregarded benefits include:

1. Public recognition

    Simply acknowledging a donor is a disregarded benefit. This acknowledgement may range from a listing in an event program to naming a building after the donor. As long as the acknowledgement does not constitute advertising, it should qualify as disregarded public recognition.

    Distinguishing between acknowledgement and advertising is not always easy. Although not directly applicable, the guidance distinguishing public recognition from advertising for the purposes of qualified sponsorship payments found in Section 513(i) of the Tax Code is helpful in distinguishing the two concepts. Public recognition includes acknowledgement of the name or logo or product lines of a trade or business. Advertising, on the other hand, includes messages containing "qualitative or comparative language, price information, or other indications of savings or value, an endorsement, or an inducement to purchase, sell, or use such products or services."[60]

2. Qualified sponsorship payments[61]

Sponsorship payments include sponsorships from corporations for an event such as a foundation's annual community awards night or golf tournament. Sponsorship payments that meet the definition of qualified sponsorship payments are fully includible as public support (subject to the 2 percent limitation) because any benefits received by the sponsor are disregarded.

Sponsorship payments that are not "qualified" are treated for the purposes of the public support test as gross receipts income or income subject to unrelated business income tax (discussed below).

Generally, a qualified sponsorship payment is defined as a payment by an individual, corporation or other entity engaged in a trade or business in which there is no agreement or expectation that the sponsor will receive any *substantial* return benefit for the sponsorship payment.[62] Therefore, to determine whether a contribution is a qualified sponsorship payment one must determine whether the benefits, if any, received in return for the contribution are substantial.

What are *insubstantial* benefits? If the only return benefit for the sponsorship payment is public recognition for the sponsor, the benefit will be deemed insubstantial. (See the previous discussion for distinguishing between public recognition and advertising.) Additionally, tax regulations have established a safe harbor defining a certain minimum amount of return benefit that is deemed insubstantial. Specifically, the fair market value of any benefits received for the sponsorship payment, such as advertising, goods or services, that does not exceed 2 percent of the total payment by the sponsor is considered insubstantial.

> *Example:* A restaurant contributes $10,000 to a community foundation to sponsor a golf tournament. If the restaurant receives up to $200 (2 percent of $10,000) in greens fees and advertising in the tournament's brochure, the sponsorship payment will still be considered a qualified sponsorship payment; the return benefit is deemed insubstantial and, thus, disregarded. (Note that while the benefits are disregarded, the amount of the contribution includible in the numerator of the public support fraction would still be subject to the 2 percent limitation discussed in Chapter 3.)

If a sponsor receives *substantial* benefits in return for its sponsorship payment, the amount equivalent to the fair market value of the benefits received will not be a qualified sponsorship payment. For the purposes of the public support test, the treatment of the portion of a payment representing the fair market value of benefits received will depend on whether the payment is income from unrelated business activities or is gross receipts income. If that portion of the payment is income from unrelated business activities, that portion will be includible in the denominator of the public support fraction as total support but not includible in the numerator as public support. If the payment is gross receipts income, the portion representing the fair market value of benefits received will be entirely excluded from the public support test calculation. In either situation, any amount that exceeds the fair market value of substantial benefits provided in return for sponsorship is

---

[60] I.R.C. § 513(i)(2)(A).

[61] Treas. Reg. 1.170A-9(e)(6)(i) defines "contributions" to include qualified sponsorship payments in the form of money or property but not services. Treas. Reg. § 1.513-4

[62] Note that the qualified sponsorship payment rules are very detailed and have multiple purposes including determining whether the payments are unrelated business taxable income.

considered a qualified sponsorship payment and thus fully includible as public support (subject to the 2 percent limitation).

> *Example*: A local restaurant contributes $10,000 to the community foundation for sponsorship of its golf tournament. The fair market value of the benefits received by the restaurant for the sponsorship is $500. Because the value of the benefits received exceeds 2 percent ($200 in this case) of the sponsorship, payment of benefits will be deemed substantial. Assuming that the tournament is run by volunteers, $500 of the $10,000 sponsorship payment will be gross receipts income. (See the discussion below to understand how to determine whether the income is gross receipts income or not.) As gross receipts income, the $500 payment would be excluded from both the numerator and the denominator of the public support fraction. The remaining $9,500 of the sponsorship payment would be includible in both the numerator and the denominator of the public support fraction. The amount includible in the numerator would be subject to the 2 percent limitation.

3. Token gifts[63]

    Disregarded benefits also include low-cost gifts provided to donors in return for their contribution. To qualify for this exception, the items provided to a donor in return for a contribution during a fundraising campaign must either be:

    a. A low-cost item (i.e., mug, keychain or t-shirt) bearing the charity's name and/or provided in return for a contribution of an amount set by the IRS.

    b. An item provided to substantial donors that does not exceed a fair market value of either an amount set by the IRS or 2 percent of the amount contributed, whichever is less.[64]

4. Membership benefits

    Certain membership benefits such as free or discounted admissions, discounted purchases in a charity's gift shop and free or discounted parking are also disregarded if they fall within certain parameters established by the IRS.[65]

Whether the return benefit to the donor is simply public recognition, a qualified sponsorship payment, a token gift or a membership benefit, the return benefit is disregarded and the full payment is includible as public support.

B. Goods and services that must be taken into account. Sometimes charities provide more than disregarded goods and services in return for a contribution. For example, if a charity holds a golf tournament to raise money, the fair market value of the round of golf, the t-shirt and the food received by the donor as a golf tournament participant does not count as a charitable contribution for the donor or as public support for the charity.[66] Any amount contributed above and beyond the value of benefits received by the donor will be a charitable contribution and public support. The portion of a donation that is actually payment for goods or services is treated either as gross receipts income or, less commonly, as income from unrelated business activity.

---

[63] IRS Publication 1771, *Charitable Contributions—Substantiation and Disclosure Requirements* (hereinafter "*Charitable Contributions*").

[64] The amounts set by the IRS are adjusted annually for inflation. In 2006, charities could give donors who contribute $43.00 or more a token item, such as a coffee mug or a t-shirt, as long as the item costs less than $8.60 and bears the charity's name or logo. Charities could provide substantial donors items having a fair market value of up to $86 or 2 percent of the amount given, whichever is less. Rev. Proc. 2005-70.

[65] See *Charitable Contributions*.

[66] The charity must provide appropriate documentation of the contribution and return benefits received if the contribution is more than $75 and the donor receives return benefits. See *Charitable Contributions* for more information.

We can work through the rules in this area using an example of the typical community foundation-sponsored golf tournament. Consider a community foundation that charges $150 to participate in its annual golf tournament. For the $150 payment, the donor may play a round of golf at the tournament valued at $40 and receives lunch valued at $20. The amount classified as "gifts, grants or contributions" would be $80, the total payment ($150) minus the $60 value of the round of golf and lunch combined. The treatment of the $60 would depend on the classification of the income as outlined below.

1. Gross receipts income

    As discussed in Chapter 4, for organizations that operate as public charities under Section 509(a)(1), gross receipts income is excluded completely from calculating the public support fraction.[67] Gross receipts include:

    a. Income generated by the charity's performance of its charitable purpose.

        A common example of gross receipts income generated from a charity's performance of its charitable purpose is ticket sales for a symphony. For community foundations, a more typical example is registration fees received for a seminar for professional advisors or workshop for local nonprofits.

    b. Income generated by nontaxable fundraising events.[68] Income from fundraising events is included under gross receipts income if the event is not taxable as unrelated business income because it is either a/an:

        ■   Event where substantially all work is performed by volunteers.

            Proceeds from donor-initiated fundraising often fall under this exception. For example, a family that raises money for a memorial fund by organizing an annual golf tournament is usually producing an event with substantially all work performed by volunteers.

        ■   Event that consists of the selling of merchandise, substantially all of which has been received by the organization as gifts or contributions.

            Proceeds from a silent auction held by the charity where all the items auctioned were donated by community members would fall under this exception.

        ■   Activity that is carried on by the organization primarily for the convenience of its members, students, patients, officers or employees.

            One example would be the operation of a dining hall on a university campus. This exception is unlikely to apply to activities of community foundations.

        ■   Bingo Game which is (1) legal under the rules of the state or locality where it is played and (2) is played in an area where bingo is not regularly carried on by for-profit companies[69]

---

[67] As mentioned earlier, charities may also meet the public support test under the gross receipts test of IRC § 509(a)(2). Under § 509(a)(2) gross receipts are included in calculating public support.

[68] See IRC § 513, Treas. Reg. 1.513-1(d) for determining whether the support is related or not to an organization's exempt purpose. Although this discussion provides an overview of some of the more frequent exceptions, it does not discuss all of the exceptions and nuances to the unrelated business income rules. See also IRS Publication 598, *Tax on Unrelated Business Income of Exempt Organizations* (available at www.irs.gov).

[69] For more information on determining whether bingo generates unrelated business income, see IRS Publication 598, *Tax on Unrelated Business Income of Exempt Organizations* (available at www.irs.gov).

It is important to note that while activities that are not regularly carried on are exempted from unrelated business income tax, income generated from these events is not considered gross receipts income; the treatment of such income is discussed below.

Returning to the golf tournament example, if the golf tournament was arranged for and run by community foundation volunteers, the $60 would be accounted for as gross receipts income for the purposes of the public support test. That means it is excluded entirely from the calculation of the public support test.

Remember: the fair market value of goods or services provided is the measuring stick for gross receipts, even where goods or services are donated. Thus, if the community foundation holds a golf tournament and provides donors with greens fees, a t-shirt and lunch, the portion of the donor's payment that equals the fair market value of these items will be gross receipts even if the golf course has donated the playing time and corporate sponsors have paid for some or all of the benefits.[70]

2. Net income from unrelated business activities

As discussed in Chapter 2, net income from unrelated business activities is included in the public support calculation whether or not the activities are carried on regularly as a trade or business. For example, payment for the golf tournament sponsored by the community foundation and run by paid staff of the community foundation or a professional event planner could fall into this category if it is not considered gross receipts income by meeting one of the definitions above. If the public charity holds fundraising events that are taxable, all income (after subtracting appropriate expenses) received as payment for the goods and services received by the donor would be included in the denominator (total support) as net income from unrelated business activity and would not be included in the numerator as public support.

Although the policy reason for such treatment of net income from unrelated business activity is unclear, one theory is that the goal of the public support test is that public support represents buy-in or oversight by the public. If support is largely from activities that are similar to those offered by commercial entities, the income is not necessarily an indicator of support and oversight by the public. Although plausible, this explanation does not explain the different treatment received by net income from unrelated business activities (included in total support but not public support) and gross receipts income (excluded from the calculation completely).

---

[70] This is also the amount that the charity must disclose on the receipt provided to event donors. See IRC § 6115, Treas. Reg. § 1.6115-1.

Figure 4: Classifying Income from Fundraising: Gross receipts income or net income from unrelated business activities?

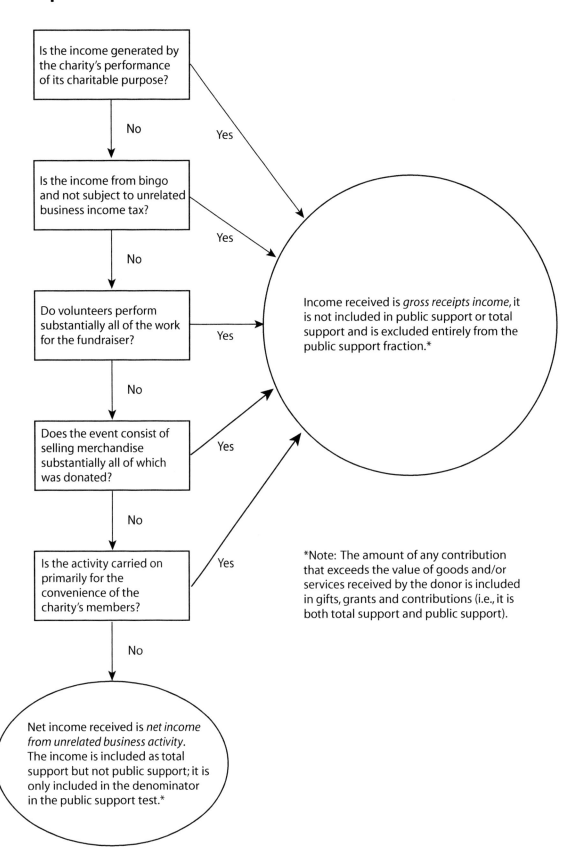

Is the income generated by the charity's performance of its charitable purpose?

No ↓ Yes →

Is the income from bingo and not subject to unrelated business income tax?

No ↓ Yes →

Do volunteers perform substantially all of the work for the fundraiser?

No ↓ Yes →

Does the event consist of selling merchandise substantially all of which was donated?

No ↓ Yes →

Is the activity carried on primarily for the convenience of the charity's members?

No ↓ Yes →

Income received is *gross receipts income*, it is not included in public support or total support and is excluded entirely from the public support fraction.*

*Note: The amount of any contribution that exceeds the value of goods and/or services received by the donor is included in gifts, grants and contributions (i.e., it is both total support and public support).

Net income received is *net income from unrelated business activity*. The income is included as total support but not public support; it is only included in the denominator in the public support test.*

© *2006, Council on Foundations, Inc.*

Below is a chart to help distinguish how income from these fundraising events is treated in the public support fraction. Remember that the portion of any donation collected that does not yield goods or services for the donor or only provides disregarded benefits in return would be reported under "gifts, grants, and contributions received" on the public support schedule.

Treatment of payments for goods and/or services

	Includible in numerator as public support	Includible in denominator as total support	Subject to 2% limitation
Gross receipts income	No	No	Not applicable
Income subject to unrelated business income tax	No	Yes	Not applicable
Qualified sponsorship payments	Yes	Yes	Yes

C. **Donor-initiated Fundraising.** Often community foundations have donors who want to raise money for a fund that these donors initially created at the foundation. These fundraisers may include golf tournaments, auctions and historic home tours. The treatment of revenue from these events hinges on whether the event is treated as a fundraising event of the community foundation itself or as an independent event carried out by the donor with proceeds donated to the community foundation. In the former case, the proceeds of the event are treated the same as with any other community foundation fundraiser; payments would typically be divided between gross receipts and contributions.

In the second case, the donor is not authorized by the community foundation to use the foundation's name and tax exemption. The donor may hold a fundraiser, but it is not a project of the community foundation and, therefore, funds raised or contributions collected by the donor are not tax deductible (unless the donor is itself a charitable organization). When the event's proceeds are turned over to the community foundation, the contribution will likely be treated by the foundation as income from the donor of the proceeds. For purposes of the public support test, whether the contribution is subject to the 2 percent limit on contributions will depend on the identity of the donor of the proceeds. For example, an individual holds a golf tournament without the approval of the community foundation. The individual collects the payment from participants (no donors to the event may take a charitable deduction). Any checks are made out to the individual. After the tournament, the individual deducts his or her expenses incurred as part of the golf tournament and contributes the remainder to the community foundation. The community foundation would likely treat the contribution as a contribution from the individual. As a contribution from an individual, the contribution would be subject to the 2 percent limit.

Other Issues Raised by Donor-initiated Fundraising

Fundraising by community foundations through special events raises more questions than just the treatment of the income for purposes of the public support test. A community foundation must ensure that it adheres to any state or local requirements for the registration for the solicitation of funds, licensing for certain activities such as raffles and collection of sales tax. These requirements often apply whether the community foundation handles the details of the events or allows a donor or group to fundraise on behalf of the community foundation.

Community foundations and other public charities must also remember their federal tax obligation to substantiate gifts in excess of $75 they receive as part contribution and part payment for goods and services. IRS Publication 1771, *Charitable Contributions—Substantiation and Disclosure Requirements* (http://www.irs.gov/pub/irs-pdf/p1771.pdf) provides more details on these requirements.

Finally, although fundraising charities are required to provide substantiation for many gifts, community foundations should not provide tax advice to donors because the tax deductibility of contributions to the community foundation may vary from donor to donor. For example, the deductibility of a contribution of box lunches by a caterer may be different than the contribution of food by an individual. The former may be a contribution of inventory subject to the special rules for inventory contributions, whereas the latter may be subject to the income tax charitable deduction rules for individuals. Also remember that a contribution of services is not deductible.

For more information on this topic, see Jane C. Nober, *Donor-Initiated Fundraising*, Second Ed., Washington, DC: Council on Foundations, 2006.

   © *2006, Council on Foundations, Inc.*

CHAPTER EIGHT

Consequences of Failing the Public Support Test

This chapter will explain the consequences if a public charity fails to pass the public support test.

What happens if a community foundation or other public charity fails the public support test? First, as noted previously, there may be a grace period during which public status can be salvaged. Second, it is not the end of the world; there are usually no tax penalties and the organization does not lose its Section 501(c)(3) status.

The basic consequence of failing the public support test is that the IRS will reclassify the organization from public charity status to private foundation status. This reclassification is not official until the IRS acts by issuing a new tax determination letter to the organization and by publishing a notice in the *Internal Revenue Bulletin* that the organization has now become a private foundation.

Back taxes and penalties may apply if the organization was new and had obtained an advance ruling letter. Under these circumstances, the excise tax on net investment income (Section 4940) will apply retroactively to the effective date of the advance ruling. Most charities will not have significant investment income, so this potential tax liability will likely be very minor. For a community foundation that builds up endowment, however, the impact may be more substantial.

Classification as a private foundation, however, will bring some unwelcome changes in the future operations of the charity. Without listing every distinction between a public charity and a private foundation, here are some of the major consequences of reclassification:

A. Added legal and accounting expenses will be necessary just to readjust.

B. A different tax return (Form 990-PF), which is somewhat more detailed and requires public disclosure of all substantial contributors, will be required.

C. Although not prohibited legally from doing so, many private foundations do not want to make grants to other private foundations because of the additional administrative time and expense required to "exercise expenditure responsibility" with its potential liability for penalty taxes. Therefore, grants from private foundations will likely not be forthcoming.

D. Living donors will be more restricted in what portion of their gifts will be deductible as charitable contributions—especially gifts of appreciated property.

E. Scholarship programs will need to be approved in advance by the IRS.

Reclassification as a private foundation is not a life sentence without parole: if circumstances change and the degree of public support begins to rebuild, it is possible to reapply to the IRS for status as a publicly supported charity.

Contributors' Reliance on an IRS Determination Letter

Under most circumstances, the status of a publicly supported organization that has failed the public support test will not officially change until written public notice of such change has been published by the IRS. As such, contributors may generally rely on a current IRS determination letter and receive a charitable deduction even if the organization is later converted to private foundation status.

The exception to this rule is that a contributor cannot rely on the current determination letter if the contributor is responsible for, or is aware of, a substantial and material change in the charity's sources of support (such as an unusually large gift). However, recognizing the chilling effect such a exception may have on grantmakers, the IRS issued guidance applicable to private foundations clarifying when a private foundation may continue to rely on an organization's determination letter.

As background, private foundations making large grants to small charities were often concerned that their grant could "tip" the public charity into private foundation status. This concern stemmed from the same sections of the regulations that permit the IRS to apply a five-year computation period in the event of a substantial and material change in the public charity's sources of support (discussed in Chapter 5). Specifically, the regulations state that a donor—including a private foundation—may not rely on an organization's letter of determination classifying the organization as a public charity if the donor is responsible for a substantial and material change in the status of the grantee. Thus, it was believed that if a private foundation's grant "tipped" a public charity into private foundation status, the granting private foundation would be subject to a tax if it had not originally taken the additional steps required when a private foundation makes a grant to another private foundation. Subsequent guidance from the IRS has clarified that unless the granting private foundation controls the public charity, it does not need to be concerned about tipping a grantee. However, some private foundations still worry about the consequences of a large grant to a small grantee. Understanding this issue can help a public charity discuss this issue with a potential private foundation funder. A more detailed discussion of this issue and a copy of IRS guidance on this issue can be found in Appendix B.

If a public charity is concerned about the impact of a large gift, it is possible for the grantee organization to request from the IRS a private letter ruling as to whether such a grant or a contribution will affect its public charity status. Any IRS ruling in response to such a request may be relied upon by grantors or contributors. However, such requests can take at least four to six months and will incur significant legal and filing costs.

Summary of the Public Support Test

The Public Support Test

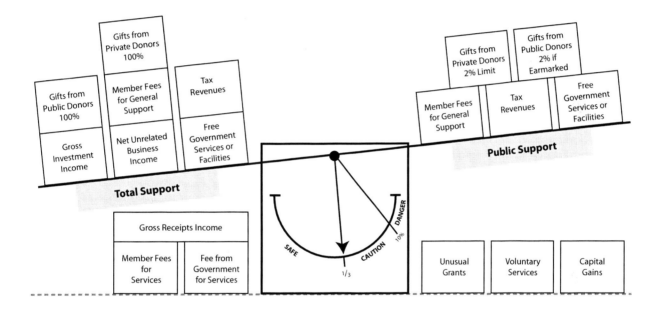

APPENDIX B

Tipping Resources

Although Chapter 8 discussed the consequences of failing the public support test from the perspective of the public charity, private foundations are often concerned about providing a grant that "tips" a public charity into private foundation status. The following article by Jane C. Nober discusses the issue of tipping from the perspective of the private foundation grantor. Revenue Procedure 89-23 (1989-1 C.B. 844) is also reproduced in this section.

© 2006, Council on Foundations, Inc.

Tipping

By Jane C. Nober [71]

Lawyers rarely tell foundation managers, "Relax, don't worry so much!" But in the case of tipping, that's been our advice for more than 10 years.

What is the so-called tipping problem and why are so many foundations (still) so worried about it?

Tipping occurs when a private foundation's support tips a public charity out of compliance with the public support test, converting it into private foundation status. Many foundation managers fear that making such a grant will lead the IRS to conclude that they have made a grant to another private foundation—a grant that would require the exercise of expenditure responsibility and compliance with the out-of-corpus rules.

In reality, Rev. Proc. 89-23 (1989-1 C.B. 844), which the Council on Foundations successfully obtained in 1989 after a ten-year effort, should eliminate almost entirely both concern about tipping and the attendant paperwork that many foundations undertake. While making big grants to a small organization can wreak havoc on the grantee's public support test calculation, foundations will generally not be held responsible for any changes their grants cause to a grantee's tax status.

Public Support, "Substantial and Material Changes"

Concern about tipping arises from the intersection of two parts of the U.S. Tax Code: the public support test and the rules about private foundation grants to other private foundations.

The Tax Code requires organizations seeking treatment as public charities based on the nature of their funding to demonstrate annually that over the past four years they have received at least one-third of their total support in contributions from the general public. The proportion of this public support can drop as low as 10 percent of total support (the total of all public support, plus endowment and other income) if the charity meets a facts and circumstances test that suggests it is trying to increase public support.

In this public support test calculation, a private foundation's grant is capped like an individual's gift—any part of the grant that is more than 2 percent of the organization's total support will not count as public support. Since all of a foundation's grant will count as total support, a big grant can decrease the proportion of funds considered public support and put a charity into private foundation status.

Before Rev. Proc. 89-23, Treasury regulations stated that a private foundation could be held responsible if its grant transformed a public charity into a private foundation. If a grantor was responsible for such a "substantial and material change" in a grantee's sources of support, it could not rely on the IRS's original determination that the grantee was a public charity. The private foundation would be required to treat the tipping grant as a grant to another private foundation. This would involve exercising expenditure responsibility (a procedure involving a pre-grant inquiry, a grant agreement and follow-up reporting) and ensuring that the out-of-corpus rules (requirements that grant funds be paid out to public charities promptly) were satisfied. Failure to undertake these procedures could result in penalty taxes.

To avoid tipping a public charity, foundation financial officers and outside counsel reviewed grantees' finances and public support calculations. When they found that a grant was likely to tip a grantee, they would require the foundation to treat the payment as a grant to another private foundation.

---

[71] This article first appeared in *Foundation News & Commentary*, Vol. 42, No. 2 (March/April 2001).

Rev. Proc. 89-23—A Safe Harbor

Rev. Proc. 89-23 was intended to free foundation staff (or counsel) from this review. The ruling provides that a foundation cannot be penalized for tipping a grantee so long as (1) the grantee has a valid IRS determination letter at the time the grant is made; (2) the IRS has not revoked the letter and the foundation is not aware of imminent action by the IRS to do so; and (3) the foundation does not control the grantee.

The safe harbor provided by Rev. Proc. 89-23 is broader than that provided by an earlier ruling, Rev. Proc. 81-6 (1981-1 C.B. 620). In that ruling, the IRS stated that it would not treat grantors as responsible for tipping long-established public charities into private foundation status if the grantor's support in any year was less than 25 percent of the aggregate support received by the grantee from all sources in the preceding four years. This position, which still required extensive review of finances, was superseded for private foundations by Rev. Proc. 89-23.

How can a foundation take advantage of the protection provided by Rev. Proc. 89-23 when making a large grant to a small organization?

First, secure a copy of the grantee's tax determination letter and verify that the organization is a public charity. In many cases, the sentence to look for states that the organization is "not a private foundation within the meaning of section 509(a) of the Internal Revenue Code" because it is described in section 509(a)(1), 509(a)(2) or 509(a)(3).

If the foundation requires a grant agreement to be signed, include a statement in which the grantee confirms its tax status as set forth in its IRS determination letter and pledges to notify the grantmaker of any change.

It is helpful for a grantmaker to inform grantees that a large grant may throw off their public support calculation and encourage them to seek other funding to offset the private foundation's support. A private foundation does not have a legal obligation to provide this information or educate its grantees about the public support test, but concerned grantmakers may wish to provide technical assistance by reviewing grantees' public support calcuations or by referring them to other resources. Foundations may consider paying large grants in installments conditioned on the grantee's meeting fundraising targets.

Grantees may be able to secure permission from the IRS to treat a foundation's grant as an unusual grant and exclude it from the public support test computation. This option, described in IRS Publication 557 as well as in Rev. Proc 81-7 (1981-1 C.B. 621), may be available when the grant (1) is attracted because of the publicly supported nature of the grantee, (2) is unexpected or unusually large and (3) would hinder the grantee in meeting the one-third public support test.

To qualify for this treatment, a grant: (1) must be made by a disinterested party, (2) may not be subject to material restrictions and (3) must be in the form of cash, marketable securities or assets that directly further the grantee's charitable activities. The IRS will consider additional factors such as the grantee's record and prospects of attracting public support.

A strong record of public support can demonstrate that an organization has generated enthusiasm for its work from the community it serves. While grantmakers may continue to examine grantees' public support history, they should keep in mind that Rev. Proc. 89-23 generally eliminates the obligation to calculate the impact of the foundation's grant and the possibility that tipping will occur.

Revenue Procedure 89-23
1989-1 C.B. 844

SECTION 1. PURPOSE

The purpose of this revenue procedure is to set forth guidelines under which grant-making private foundations will not be considered to be responsible for substantial and material changes in the sources of financial support of recipient organizations that are described in sections 170(b)(1)(A)(vi) or 509(a)(2) of the Internal Revenue Code.

SEC. 2. BACKGROUND

01. Generally, under section 1.170A-9(e)(4)(v)(b), 1.170A- 9(e)(5)(iii)(c), 1.509(a)-3(c)(l)(iii), and 1.509(a)-3(e)-(3) of the Income Tax Regulations, when an organization has received a ruling or determination letter, or an advance ruling or determination letter, that it has been classified as a publicly supported organization described in sections 170(b)(1)-(A)(vi) or 509(a)(2) of the Code, the treatment of grants and contributions and the status of grantors and contributors to the organization under sections 170, 507, 545(b)(2), 556(b)(2), 642(c), 4942, 4945, 2055, 2106(a)(2), and 2522 will not be affected by a subsequent loss of classification as publicly supported organization until notice of loss of classification is published. However, a grantor or contributor may not rely on such an organization's classification if the grantor or contributor is responsible for or aware of a substantial and material change in the organization's sources of support that subsequently results in the organization's loss of classification as a publicly supported organization. For example, a substantial and material change in sources of support may result from the receipt of an unusually large contribution that does not qualify as an unusual grant under sections 1.170A-9(e)(6)(ii) or 1.509(a)-3(c)(3). See Sec. 2.01 of Rev. Proc. 81-6, 1981-1 C.B. 620.

02. If any taxable year there is a substantial and material change in an organization's sources of support, the computation period used to determine whether the organization meets the requirements of the section 170(b)(1)(A)-(vi) or 509(a)(2) financial support tests consists of the taxable year in question and the four immediately preceding taxable years rather than the four immediately preceding taxable years. If an organization has been in existence for less than five taxable year, the computation period consists of the taxable year in question and the number of years preceding that taxable year that the organization has been in existence. This computation period is in lieu of the usual computation period rules. See sections 1.170A-9(e)-(4)(v) and 1.509(a)-3(c)(l)(ii) of the regulations and Sec. 2.02 of Rev. Proc. 81-6.

03. Gifts, grants and contributions made by a private foundation to another private foundation are not qualifying distributions under section 4942(g) of the Code unless the recipient is either (i) an operating foundation under section 4942(j)(3) or (ii) a pass-through foundation under section 4942(g)(3) from which the grantor obtains the records required by section 4942(g)(3)(B). Therefore, a private foundation may not be able to count a grant, for instance, as a qualifying distribution if the grant causes the recipient organization to lose its classification as a public charity.

04. Gifts, grants and contributions made by a private foundation to another private foundation are taxable expenditures under section 4945(d)(4) of the Code unless either (i) the recipient is an exempt operating foundation under section 4940(d)(2) or (ii) the grantor exercises expenditure responsibility under section 4945(h). Therefore, a private foundation may be subject to the section 4945(a) tax on taxable expenditures if it has not followed the expenditure responsibility requirements of section 4945(d)(4) in regard to a grant that causes the recipient organization to lose its classification as a public charity.

    © *2006, Council on Foundations, Inc.*

05. Rev. Proc. 81-6 set forth guidelines under which a grantor or contributor will not be considered to be responsible for substantial and material changes in a organization's sources of support. Generally, these guidelines provide that a grantor or contributor will not be considered to be responsible for a substantial and material change in an organization's support if the aggregate of gifts, grants, or contributions received from such grantor or contributor for a taxable year is 25 percent or less of the aggregate support received by the donee organization from all sources other than that donor for the four taxable years immediately preceding such taxable year, or, if the donee organization has been in existence for fewer than five taxable years, the number of years for which the organization has been in existence prior to the taxable year being tested.

06. In 1984, Congress directed the Treasury Department to amend its regulations to permit greater reliance by private foundations on Internal Revenue Service classifications of new organizations in the first five years of their existence and in any other circumstances in which Treasury concludes that greater reliance is appropriate. H.R. Conf. Rep. No. 861, 98th Cong., 2d Sess. 1090 (1984), 1984-3 (Vol. 2) C.B. 344, Pending the issuance of regulations implementing the above directions, the Internal Revenue Service will follow the guidelines set forth below.

SEC. 3. GUIDELINES

01. Private foundations may continue to rely on the status of recipient organizations that have received rulings or determination letters to the extent provided in sections 1.170A-9(e)(4)(v)(b) and 1.509(a)-3(c)(l)(iii) of the regulations, and on the status of recipient organizations that have received advance rulings or determination letters to the extent provided in sections 1.170A- 9(e)-(5)(iii)(c) and 1.509(a)-3(e)(3).

02. All grantors and contributors, including private foundations, may continue to rely on the guidelines set forth in Rev. Proc. 81-6.

03. In addition, a private foundation's gift, grant or contribution will not cause the private foundation to be considered to be responsible for, or aware of, a substantial and material change in the recipient organization's sources of support that results in the loss of the recipient organization's status under sections 170(b)(A)(vi) or 509(a)(2) of the Code if the following conditions are met at the time of the making of the gift, grant or contribution:

(1) The recipient organization has received a ruling or determination letter, or an advance ruling or determination letter, that it is described in sections 170(b)(1)(A)(vi) or 509(a)(2);

(2) Notice of a change of the recipient organization's status under sections 170(b)(1)(A)(vi) or 509(a)(2) has not been made to the public (such as by publication in the Internal Revenue Bulletin), and the private foundation has not acquired knowledge that the Internal Revenue Service has given notice to the recipient organization that it will be deleted from such status; and

(3) The recipient organization is not controlled directly or indirectly by the private foundation. A recipient organization is controlled by a private foundation for this purpose if the private foundation and disqualified persons (defined in section 4946(a)(1)(A) through (G)) with reference to the private foundation, by aggregating their votes or positions of authority may require the recipient organization to perform any act which significantly affects its operations or may prevent the recipient organization from performing such act.

SEC. 4 AREAS NOT COVERED BY THIS REVENUE PROCEDURE

01. This revenue procedure does not apply to situations in which gifts, grants, or contributions are made by persons other than private foundations.

02. This revenue procedure does not affect Rev. Proc. 81-7, 1981-1 C.B. 621, under which grants will be considered to be unusual grants.

SEC. 5 EFFECT ON OTHER DOCUMENTS

Rev. Proc. 81-6, 1981-1 C.B. 620, is amplified.

SEC. 6. EFFECTIVE DATE

This revenue procedure is effective for grants made after March 13, 1989.

DRAFTING INFORMATION

The principal author of this revenue procedure is V. Moore of the Office of Assistant Chief Counsel (Employee Benefits and Exempt Organizations). For further information regarding this revenue procedure contact Robert Fontenrose on (202) 566-4134 (not a toll- free call).

© *2006, Council on Foundations, Inc.*

Appendix C

Unusual Grants

Revenue Procedure 81-7 (1981-1 C.B. 621)

Section 1. Purpose

The purpose of this revenue procedure is to set forth guidelines as to the grants or contributions that will be considered "unusual grants" under sections 1.170A-9(e)(6)(ii) and 1.509(a)-3(c)(3) and related provisions of the Income Tax Regulations without benefit of an advance ruling from the Internal Revenue Service. These guidelines are intended to provide advance assurance to grantors and contributors that they will not be considered to be responsible for "substantial and material" changes in sources of financial support for purposes of sections 1.170A-9(e)(4)(v)(b) and 1.509(a)-3(c)(1)(iii).

Sec. 2. Background

.01 Sections 1.170A-9(e)(4)(v)(b) and 1.509(a)-3(c)(1)(iii) of the regulations state that once an organization has been classified as a publicly supported organization described in section 170(b)(1)(A)(vi) or 509(a)(2) of the Internal Revenue Code, the treatment of grants and contributions and the status of grantors and contributors to the organization under sections 170, 507, 545(b)(2), 556(b)(2), 642(c), 4942, 4945, 2055, 2106(a)(2), and 2522 will not be affected by a subsequent loss of classification as a publicly supported organization until notice of loss of classification is published. However, a grantor or contributor may not rely on such an organization's classification if the grantor or contributor is responsible for or aware of a "substantial and material" change in the organization's sources of support that subsequently results in the organization's loss of classification as a publicly supported organization. For example, a "substantial and material" change in sources of support may result from the receipt of an unusually large contribution that does not qualify as an unusual grant under section 1.170A-9(e)(6)(ii) or 1.509(a)-3(c)(3). The contributor, even though he or she relied on a letter classifying the organization as a section 170(b)(1)(A)(vi) or 509(a)(2) organization, may not receive the benefit of the deduction limits under sections 170(b)(1)(A)(vi) and 170(b)(1)(A)(viii) if as a result of his or her contribution the organization loses its classification as a public charity. Similarly, a grant-making private foundation might find itself subject to the section 4945(a) tax on taxable expenditures because it may not have followed expenditure responsibility requirements of section 4945(d)(4) of the Code for grants to non-public organizations if its grant is not an unusual grant and the grantee organization loses its classification as a public charity.

.02 The receipt of an "unusual grant" as defined in sections 1.170A-9(e)(6)(ii) and 1.509(a)-3(c)(3) of the regulations will not cause a "substantial and material" change within the meaning of sections 1.170A-9(e)(4)(v)(b) and 1.509(a)-3(c)(1)(iii). Thus, a grantor or contributor who makes a grant or contribution which is an "unusual grant" to a section 170(b)(1)(A)(vi) or 509(a)(2) organization will not be responsible for a "substantial and material" change in that organization's sources of support.

Sec. 3. Guidelines

.01 A grant or contribution with all of the following characteristics, derived from the factors contained in section 1.509(a)-3(c)(4) regarding whether a particular contribution is an unusual grant will be considered an unusual grant if by reason of its size it adversely affects the status of an organization under section 170(b)(1)(A)(vi) or 509(a)(2) of the Code within the meaning of sections 1.170A-9(e)(6)(ii) and 1.509(a)-3(c)(3):

1 The grant or contribution is made by a person other than a person (or persons standing in a relationship described in section 4946(a)(1)(C) through (G) to that person) who created the organization or was a substantial contributor to the organization within the meaning of section 507(d)(2) prior to the grant or contribution.

2 The grant or contribution is not made by a person (or persons standing in a relationship described in section 4946(a)(1)(C) through (G) to that person) who is in a position of authority such as a foundation manager (within the meaning of section 4946(b)) with respect to the organization or who otherwise has the ability to exercise control over the organization. Similarly, the grant or contribution is not made by a person (or persons standing in a relationship described in section 4946(a)(1)(C) through (G) to that person) who, as a consequence of a grant or contribution, obtains a position of authority or the ability to otherwise exercise control over the organization.

3 The grant or contribution is in the form of cash, readily marketable securities, or assets that directly further the exempt purposes of the organization, such as a gift of a painting to a museum.

4 The donee-organization has received either an advance or final ruling or determination letter classifying it as an organization described in section 170(b)(1)(A)(vi) or 509(a)(2) and, except in the case of an organization operating under an advance ruling or determination letter, the organization is actively engaged in a program of activities in furtherance of its exempt purpose.

5 No material restrictions or conditions (within the meaning of section 1.507-2(a)(8)) have been imposed by the grantor or contributor upon the organization in connection with the grant or contribution.

6 If the grant or contribution is intended to underwrite operating expenses, as opposed to financing capital items, the terms and amount of the grant or contribution are expressly limited to underwriting no more than one year's operating expenses.

.02 A grant or contribution will adversely affect the status of an organization under section 170(b)(1)(A)(vi) or 509(a)(2) within the meaning of Sec. 3.01 only if the organization otherwise meets the support test described in section 170(b)(1)(A)(vi) or 509(a)(2) in the year being tested without benefit of the grant or contribution.

.03 Notwithstanding Sec. 3.01, a potential grantee organization may request a ruling under Rev. Proc. 80-24, 1980-1 C.B. 658, on whether a proposed grant or contribution with or without the above characteristics will constitute an unusual grant, as provided for in sections 1.509(a)-3(c)(5)(ii) and 1.170A-9(e)(6)(iv)(b).

Sec. 4. Examples

The following examples illustrate the guidelines in Sec. 3.

.01 During the years 1975-1978, A, a section 509(a)(2) organization, received aggregate support of $350,000. Of this amount, $105,000 was received from grants, contributions and receipts from admissions that are described in sections 509(a)(2)(A)(i) and (ii). An additional $150,000 was received from grants and contributions from substantial contributors described in section 507(d)(2) of the Code (disqualified persons under section 4946(a)(1)(A)). The remaining $95,000 was gross investment income as defined in section 509(e) of the Code. Included in the contributions from disqualified persons was a contribution of $50,000 from X. X was not a substantial contributor to the organization prior to the making of this contribution. In addition, all of the other requirements of Sec.

3.01 were met with respect to X's contribution. If X's contribution is excluded from A's support by reason of the fact that it is an unusual grant, A will have received, for the years 1975-1978, $105,000 from sources described in sections 509(a)(2)(A)(i) and (ii), $100,000 in grants and contributions from disqualified persons, and $95,000 in gross investment income. Therefore, if X's contribution is excluded from A's support, A meets the requirements of the section 509(a)(2) support test for the year 1979 because more than one-third of its support is from sources described in sections 509(a)(2)(A)(i) and (ii) and no more than one-third of its support is gross investment income. Thus, X's contribution adversely affects the status of A within the meaning of Sec. 3.02 and since the guidelines of Sec. 3.01 are met, the contribution is excludable as an unusual grant. X will not be considered responsible for a "substantial and material" change in A's support.

The computations to show the effect of excluding X's contribution from A's support are as follows:

Aggregate support received by A during
the tax years from 1975 through 1978 _____$350,000

Less: Contribution from X _____ 50,000
                                                                    _____
Aggregate support of A less contribution from X _____$300,000

Gross investment income received by A as a percentage of A's total
support (less the contribution of $50,000 from X)_____ $95,00
                                                                        _____ = 31.67%
                                                                        $300,000

Grants, contributions, and receipts from admissions described
in sections 509(a)(2)(i) and (ii) received by A as a percentage of
A's aggregate support (less the contribution of $50,000 from X) _____ $105,000
                                                                             _____ = 35%
                                                                             $300,000

.02 Under the same facts, except that for the years 1975-1978, A received $100,000 from grants or contributions from disqualified persons instead of $150,000, the result would be different. In this case, if X's contribution is excluded as an unusual grant, A will have received $105,000 from sources that are described in sections 509(a)(2)(A)(i) and (ii), $50,000 in grants and contributions from disqualified persons, and $95,000 in gross investment income. If X's contribution is excluded from A's support, A will have received more than one-third of its support from gross investment income and A would not meet the requirements of the section 509(a)(2) support test for the year 1979. Thus, even though all the requirements of Sec. 3.01 are met with respect to X's contribution, it is not excludable as an unusual grant because it does not adversely affect the status of A within the meaning of Sec. 3.02.

The computations to show the effect of excluding X's contribution from A's support are as follows:

Aggregate support received by A during the tax years 1975 through 1978 _____ $300,000

Less: Contribution from X _____ 50,000

Aggregate support of A less contribution from X _____ $250,000

Gross investment income received by A as a percentage of A's
total support (less the contribution of $50,000 from X) _____ $95,000

$250,000

= 38%

    © 2006, Council on Foundations, Inc.

Appendix D

Calculating the Public Support Test Using Form 990, Schedule A

As mentioned before, the primary mechanism for reporting an organization's public support percentage is Schedule A of IRS Form 990. This schedule requires publicly supported charities to list all sources of revenue for the appropriate four-year calculation period. The information is provided in Part IV-A by completing a Support Schedule on Lines 15 through 26. (Note that organizations qualifying as public charities under the second public support test described in Section 509(a)(2) of the Internal Revenue Code do not complete line 26 but instead demonstrate that they meet the application test by completing line 27.)

On the next page is a copy of the Support Schedule from Schedule A of the Form 990. Working with this form should help put the information contained within this publication into concrete terms.

Note that the form (in this case for the 2005 tax year) sets forth the years upon which the test will be calculated. Lines 15–22 of the form are the lines where income is listed for the applicable four-year period. Lines 23–25 provide instructions to perform calculations.

Line 26 embodies the actual computation of the public support test. Line 26f allows for individuals to take a quick look at the schedule and determine the organization's percentage of public support. If an organization is relying on the facts and circumstances test, the organization should also attach a statement setting forth the facts and circum-stances on which it is relying to meet the test.

The copy of the Support Schedule from Schedule A of the Form 990 on the next page, the appropriate line items (boxes) have been identified with uppercase letters to demonstrate how the numbers work together to obtain an organization's percentage of public support.

$$\frac{(A\text{-}L) + B + F + G}{A + B + D + E + F + G + H} = \text{Percentage of Public Support}$$

Of special note is that while an organization is required to maintain a list showing the name of and amount con-tributed by each donor (other than publicly supported organizations or governmental units) whose total gifts exceed 2 percent of the organization's total support (found on line 26a), this information is not submitted to the IRS. Instead, this information should be kept on file by the organization. Similarly, documentation of any unusual grants should be kept consistent with the instructions on line 28 but does not have to be submitted to the IRS with the return.

Part IV-A Support Schedule (Complete only if you checked a box on line 10, 11, or 12.) *Use cash method of accounting.*

Note: *You may use the worksheet in the instructions for converting from the accrual to the cash method of accounting.*

Calendar year (or fiscal year beginning in) ▶	(a) 2004	(b) 2003	(c) 2002	(d) 2001	(e) Total
15 Gifts, grants, and contributions received. (Do not include unusual grants. See line 28.) .					**A**
16 Membership fees received					**B**
17 Gross receipts from admissions, merchandise sold or services performed, or furnishing of facilities in any activity that is related to the organization's charitable, etc., purpose . .					**C**
18 Gross income from interest, dividends, amounts received from payments on securities loans (section 512(a)(5)), rents, royalties, and unrelated business taxable income (less section 511 taxes) from businesses acquired by the organization after June 30, 1975 .					**D**
19 Net income from unrelated business activities not included in line 18. . . .					**E**
20 Tax revenues levied for the organization's benefit and either paid to it or expended on its behalf					**F**
21 The value of services or facilities furnished to the organization by a governmental unit without charge. Do not include the value of services or facilities generally furnished to the public without charge					**G**
22 Other income. Attach a schedule. Do not include gain or (loss) from sale of capital assets					**H**
23 Total of lines 15 through 22					**I**
24 Line 23 minus line 17					**J**
25 Enter 1% of line 23					

26 **Organizations described on lines 10 or 11:**   **a** Enter 2% of amount in column (e), line 24 . . . . ▶   **26a**   **K**

   b Prepare a list for your records to show the name of and amount contributed by each person (other than a governmental unit or publicly supported organization) whose total gifts for 2001 through 2004 exceeded the amount shown in line 26a. **Do not file this list with your return.** Enter the total of all these excess amounts ▶   **26b**   **L**

   c Total support for section 509(a)(1) test: Enter line 24, column (e) . . . . ▶   **26c**

   d Add: Amounts from column (e) for lines: 18 _____   19 _____
                                      22 _____   26b _____   . . . . . ▶   **26d**

   e Public support (line 26c minus line 26d total) . . . . ▶   **26e**

   f **Public support percentage (line 26e (numerator) divided by line 26c (denominator))** . . . . . ▶   **26f**   %

27 **Organizations described on line 12:**   **a** For amounts included in lines 15, 16, and 17 that were received from a "disqualified person," prepare a list for your records to show the name of, and total amounts received in each year from, each "disqualified person." **Do not file this list with your return.** Enter the sum of such amounts for each year:

    (2004) .... (2003) .... (2002) .... (2001) ....

   b For any amount included in line 17 that was received from each person (other than "disqualified persons"), prepare a list for your records to show the name of, and amount received for each year, that was more than the **larger** of **(1)** the amount on line 25 for the year or **(2)** $5,000. (Include in the list organizations described in lines 5 through 11b, as well as individuals.) **Do not file this list with your return.** After computing the difference between the amount received and the larger amount described in **(1)** or **(2)**, enter the sum of these differences (the excess amounts) for each year:

    (2004) .... (2003) .... (2002) .... (2001) ....

   c Add: Amounts from column (e) for lines: 15 _____   16 _____
                            17 _____   20 _____   21 _____   . . . . . . ▶   **27c**

   d Add: Line 27a total. _____   and line 27b total . _____   . . . . . . ▶   **27d**

   e Public support (line 27c total minus line 27d total) . . . . ▶   **27e**

   f Total support for section 509(a)(2) test: Enter amount from line 23, column (e) . . ▶   **27f**

   g **Public support percentage (line 27e (numerator) divided by line 27f (denominator))** . . . . . ▶   **27g**   %

   h **Investment income percentage (line 18, column (e) (numerator) divided by line 27f (denominator)).** ▶   **27h**   %

28 **Unusual Grants:** For an organization described in line 10, 11, or 12 that received any unusual grants during 2001 through 2004, prepare a list for your records to show, for each year, the name of the contributor, the date and amount of the grant, and a brief description of the nature of the grant. **Do not file this list with your return.** Do not include these grants in line 15.